SOUTH KOREA

BY ALEXIS BURLING

Essential Library

An Imprint of Abdo Publishing
abdobooks.com

ABDOBOOKS.COM
Published by Abdo Publishing, a division of ABDO, PO Box 398166, Minneapolis, Minnesota 55439.

Printed in China.
052025
092025

Cover Photo: C. J. Nattanai/Shutterstock Images (pavilion); Shutterstock Images (pattern)
Interior Photos: Joshua Davenport/Shutterstock Images, 4–5; Nattee Chalermtiragool/Shutterstock Images, 7; Shutterstock Images, 8, 10, 13, 18 (globe), 21, 37, 47, 53, 56, 70, 84, 85, 86–87, 101; Yao Qilin/Xinhua/Alamy Live News/Alamy, 14–15; Sanga Park/Shutterstock Images, 16–17; Red Line Editorial, 18 (map); Ju Namy/Shutterstock Images, 19; Sayan Uranan/Shutterstock Images, 24; Gudkov Andrey/Shutterstock Images, 26–27; P. Tomlins/Alamy, 29; Suvorov Alex/Shutterstock Images, 32; MichaelGrantWildlife/Alamy, 34; Eric Isselee/Shutterstock Images, 36; Pictures from History/CPA Media Pte Ltd./Alamy, 38–39; US Army/Archive Photos/Getty Images, 40; Pictures from History/Universal Images Group/Getty Images, 44; Chung Sung-Jun/Getty Images News/Getty Images, 48, 67; Emma McIntyre/Getty Images for Coachella/Getty Images Entertainment/Getty Images, 50–51; Panwasin Seemala/Shutterstock Images, 55; Cindy Ord/WireImage/Getty Images, 59; Samir Hussein/WireImage/Getty Images, 60; Universal History Archive/Universal Images Group/Getty Images, 62–63; Daniel Fung/Shutterstock Images, 64; Kim Min-Hee/AFP/Getty Images, 69; Drew Angerer/Getty Images News/Getty Images, 72; Seokyong Lee/Bloomberg/Getty Images, 74–75; SeongJoon Cho/Bloomberg/Getty Images, 77; Liesa Johannssen/Bloomberg/Getty Images, 78; Jon Chica/Shutterstock Images, 82–83; Art Directors & Trip/Alamy, 88; Jean Chung/Bloomberg/Getty Images, 93; Daily Travel Photos/Alamy, 94; Chris Jung/NurPhoto/Getty Images, 97; Panya Khamtuy/Alamy, 98–99

Editor: Marley Richmond
Series Designer: Maggie Villaume

Library of Congress Control Number: 2024948585

PUBLISHER'S CATALOGING-IN-PUBLICATION DATA
Names: Burling, Alexis, author.
Title: South Korea / by Alexis Burling
Description: Minneapolis, Minnesota: Abdo Publishing, 2026 | Series: Essential library of countries | Includes online resources and index.
Identifiers: ISBN 9781098297022 (lib. bdg.) | ISBN 9798384919544 (ebook)
Subjects: LCSH: Geography--Juvenile literature. | Korea (South)--Juvenile literature. | Asia--Juvenile literature. | Korea (South)--History--Juvenile literature.
Classification: DDC 951.95--dc23

CONTENTS

CHAPTER **ONE**

A TOUR OF SOUTH KOREA

The trip Min-ho Kang had been looking forward to since he was a young boy was here. For his fifteenth birthday, his parents were taking him and his younger sister, Jin-hee, on a tour of their favorite places in South Korea. The highlight of the vacation would be a few days in Seoul, South Korea's capital, situated along the Han River. Min-ho couldn't wait to explore the city's historic palaces, sacred Buddhist temples, bustling street markets, and more.

After visiting Seoul, the Kangs would take a quick flight to South Korea's port city of Busan. Busan was where Min-ho's parents had grown up and where some of his aunts and uncles still lived. Min-ho was excited to see the city's beaches.

Seoul is the cultural center of South Korea. The city is home to many museums, libraries, and theaters.

As the plane made its descent toward Incheon International Airport, South Korea's main airport, Min-ho could barely contain his excitement. From above he could see a skyline full of towering, glittering skyscrapers of all shapes and sizes. It all looked vastly different than the cornfields of Iowa where he and his family lived in the United States. Min-ho was looking forward to discovering everything South Korea had to offer.

BUILDINGS BIG AND TALL

When the hotel alarm clock blared at seven o'clock the next morning, Min-ho jumped out of bed, threw on some clothes, and was ready to go. His father had already gone out and stopped at a street vendor down the block from the hotel to pick up some coffee and *gilgeori* toast for everyone to start the day. Gilgeori toast is made with two slices of buttery milk bread. The sandwich contains egg, cabbage, carrots, green onion, ham, and cheese with a dash of ketchup. It was exactly what Min-ho needed to get his energy flowing for the day ahead.

The Kangs' first stop of the day was the majestic Gyeongbokgung Palace, a massive compound of cobblestone courtyards and ornate pagodas decorated in green, white, and red. The palace was hidden behind the traditional two-story pavilion and three arched gateways of Gwanghwamun Gate. Built in 1395, Gyeongbokgung Palace was the main palace and government seat of the Joseon dynasty, the royal family who ruled the Korean Peninsula from 1392 to 1910.

Min-ho learned that most of the palace's original structures had been destroyed and reconstructed twice. The first destruction occurred in a fire during the Imjin War (1592–1598) with

Geunjeongjeon Hall, Gyeongbokgung Palace's main hall, was first built in 1394. The current building was reconstructed in 1867.

Japan, and the other happened during Japan's occupation of South Korea in the 1900s. After some of the 330 buildings were restored to their former glory during the 1990s, Gyeongbokgung Palace became one of the most popular tourist destinations in South Korea.[1] The Kangs saw that some visitors wore rented traditional Korean outfits called *hanbok*, which earned them free admission.

At ten o'clock, the Kangs watched the hour-long ceremony at Gwanghwamun Gate. Men dressed in vibrant red, blue, and yellow replica uniforms marched around the courtyard and reenacted the traditional changing of the guard. Then the family took a guided tour of the palace and grounds. Min-ho's favorite stop was Geunjeongjeon Hall. With a huge red-and-gold throne at the back of the room and a ceiling of intricately carved stone and wood, it was easy for Min-ho to imagine the South Korean king conducting his business there.

Jin-hee gravitated toward the two-story, hexagonal Hyangwonjeong Pavilion. Nearby there was a reflection pond topped with dozens of lotus flowers, the ancient Korean symbol of rebirth. She thought the pavilion, made entirely of stone and painted wood, was the perfect example of beauty.

After the tour, the Kangs were so hungry that they ordered nearly a dozen dishes for lunch, including *samgyetang*, a Korean ginseng chicken soup, and *japchae*, a stir-fry made with cellophane noodles, pork, and vegetables. Min-ho devoured

HANBOK

Hanbok is the name for the traditional clothing of Korea. Characterized by vibrant colors, elegant designs, and delicate embroidery, these garments have a history that dates back thousands of years. Women's hanbok are made of two parts. The jacket or blouse, called a *jeogori*, is usually cropped and slightly oversized. It has wide sleeves and a rounded collar. The skirt, called a *chima*, is high waisted and flows down to the ankles. The set is joined together by a wide sash called a *goreum*. Men's hanbok consist of a longer jeogori and wide-legged *baji*, or pants, that are tied at the waist and ankles with string.

SEOUL'S SUBWAY SYSTEM

People in Seoul can navigate the city's bustling streets and neighborhoods using its public transportation system. There are plenty of taxis and buses available, but many locals use the subway, also called the metro. It is considered one of the cleanest, most punctual, and easiest-to-use subways in the world. Trains run from 5:30 a.m. until midnight, and all are equipped with free Wi-Fi. There are 22 lines, which are color coded and make 302 stops around the city. Station signs are written in Korean, English, Japanese, and Chinese. Fares start at 1,400 South Korean won, or approximately one US dollar, per ride.[2]

the rice cakes, eggs, and dumplings in the *tteokguk*'s delicious broth. Jin-hee's favorite was the *chuncheon dakgalbi* made with chunks of chicken, rice cakes, and vegetables marinated in a chili-paste sauce.

With their stomachs full, the Kangs took a subway to Lotte World Tower, the tallest building in South Korea. Min-ho and his family spent hours going through the exhibits in the glass-floored Seoul Sky Observatory at the top of the structure. The exhibits explained the history behind some of the famous landmarks throughout the city.

Looking down from above, they could see the park where the 1988 Summer Olympics were held, Seoul's glitzy Gangnam shopping district, and the meandering Han River. The scariest part was the outside walk over the tower's sky bridge, a metal walking bridge suspended between the two sides of the skyscraper's split top. The Kangs were given helmets, special windproof suits, and harnesses to wear. Workers clipped them to an overhead rail to prevent anyone from falling. After the outside tour, the Kangs had a lighter meal in one of the tower's restaurants before heading back to the hotel.

The *hanok* of Bukchon Village are constructed with tiled roofs, stone floors, red pine accents, and brick or stone walls.

A TRIP BACK IN TIME

Standing at a height of 1,821 feet (555 m) and including 123 stories, Lotte World Tower is the world's sixth-tallest building.[5]

On day two of their itinerary, the Kangs began their day with a traditional Korean breakfast. The family traded helpings of typical dishes such as *gyeran bap*, Korean rice flavored with soy sauce and sesame oil and topped with fried egg; *miyeokguk*, seaweed soup with beef; and grilled mackerel. They then took the subway to Bukchon Village, a charming neighborhood between Gyeongbokgung Palace and Changdeok Palace in north-central Seoul.

From his research, Min-ho knew that Bukchon Village was famous for being the largest collection of traditional Korean homes, called *hanok*, in the country. Some were up to 600 years old. These 900 structures were some of the most beautiful buildings Min-ho had ever seen.[3] Some had been converted into tea shops or restaurants. Others had become art galleries or museums. Still others remained privately owned by multiple generations of the same Korean families and were still used as homes.

Jin-hee loved the boutique she passed where customers could create a perfume based on their emotions. Mr. Kang spent more than an hour exploring the Gahoe Museum, which showcased more than 250 Korean folk paintings, 750 ancient amulets used to ward off evil, 150 classical books, and 200 traditional folding screens that had once been used as room separators.[4] Mrs. Kang's top pick was the Han Sangsu Embroidery Museum, which displayed delicately woven works by world-renowned craftspeople. As for Min-ho, he couldn't stop thinking with his stomach.

His favorite stop was the hour-long traditional Korean cooking workshop held at the Museum of Korean Art.

After a full day walking the cobblestone streets of Bukchon, the Kangs were exhausted from all the activities. They made a few stops at street vendors for beef skewers and grilled rice balls. But before they called the day complete, the family made one more stop: the Seoul Lantern Festival.

This two-week event takes place every November along the Cheonggyecheon Stream in the center of Seoul. The celebration is the largest Korean lantern festival in the country. Hundreds of LED lanterns line the stream along with even more traditional candlelit lanterns, all designed by local and international artists. The festival is known around the world as a celebration of South Korean history and culture. Since its inception in 2009, the Seoul Lantern Festival has attracted more than two million visitors every year.[6]

Before Min-ho and his family got back on a plane to travel south to Busan and stay with their family, they spent the next few days of their trip visiting more of the many places Seoul had to offer.

A TOO-POPULAR DESTINATION

Similarly to many popular tourist destinations all over the world, Bukchon Village sees thousands of visitors every day. As a result, many of the 6,000 people who live there are growing tired of the noise, street traffic, and litter that they say are ruining the neighborhood.[7] In 2018 signs were hung that warned tourists to keep noise levels low. In 2024 local officials announced plans to enact curfews for nonresidents in certain areas. Under these new rules, tourists cannot access these areas between 5:00 p.m. and 10:00 a.m. Large buses are prohibited from traveling through these areas as well. Anyone violating these restrictions can be fined.

Dongdaemun Market is known for its delicious and inexpensive street food.

Min-ho's favorite stops were Changdeokgung, another royal palace; Jongmyo, the royal ancestral shrine of the Joseon dynasty; and Dongdaemun Market, a shopping district that stretched for ten city blocks.[8] Jin-hee and her mom preferred Seoul's natural spaces, which were perfect for finding peace and calm. Bukhansan National Park, a 30-square-mile (78 sq km) park full of granite peaks, forests, and dozens of hiking trails, was one place they hoped to see again.[9]

Gangneung Danoje Festival is one of South Korea's oldest folk traditions. The mask dance performed as part of the festival depicts folk stories.

A MAGNIFICENT COUNTRY

From Seoul to Busan and beyond, South Korea is a fascinating country with a complicated history. Since the Korean War (1950–1953) ended, South Korea has been formally separated from North Korea. South Korea has tried to maintain peace with its neighbor to the north while also weathering periods of political instability within its own borders.

Still, South Korea boasts a world-renowned culture today. It is home to mouth-watering cuisine, world-famous music and beauty trends, leading technology and electronics industries, and deep spiritual traditions. With a thriving economy and top-of-the-line public transit system, the country has become not only one of the top tourist destinations in the world but also a rewarding place for South Koreans to live.

CHAPTER **TWO**

GEOGRAPHY

Korea is a peninsula that is about 600 miles (966 km) long.[1] It is located on the eastern coast of Asia. South Korea borders the Democratic People's Republic of Korea, commonly known as North Korea, to the north; the Sea of Japan to the east; the East China Sea to the south; and the Yellow Sea to the west. The Korean Strait borders the country to the southeast, separating the East China Sea and the Sea of Japan. South Korea has an area of 38,502 square miles (99,720 sq km).[2] That is slightly smaller than the size of Pennsylvania in the United States.

South Korea has a diverse landscape. The land is made of rock that is more than 540 million years old.[3] The geography of the country consists of volcanic islands, dense urban areas, mountains, wide coastal plains, and a small area of jungle in the south.

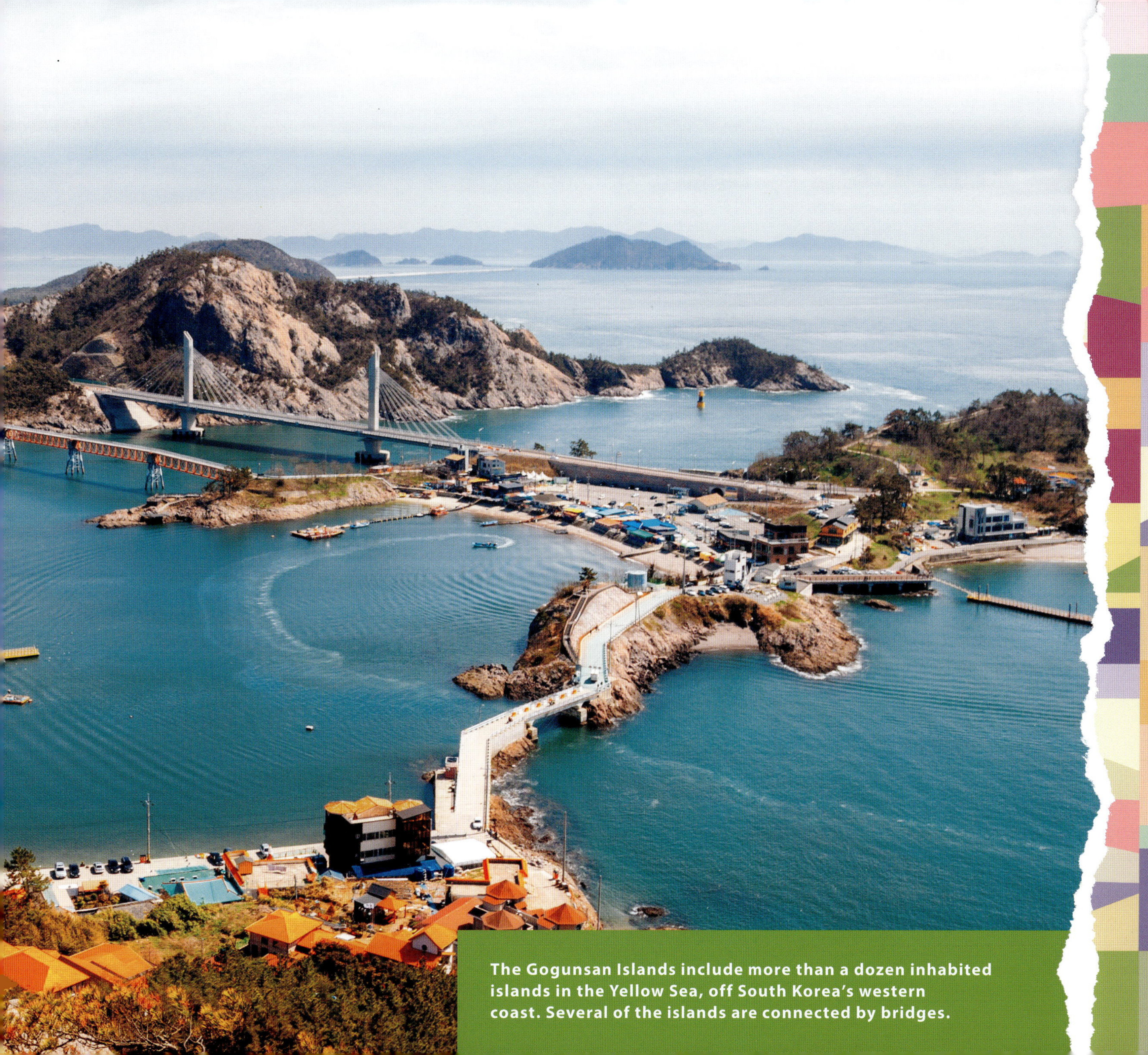

The Gogunsan Islands include more than a dozen inhabited islands in the Yellow Sea, off South Korea's western coast. Several of the islands are connected by bridges.

MAP OF SOUTH KOREA

KEY:
- Capital
- City
- Point of Interest

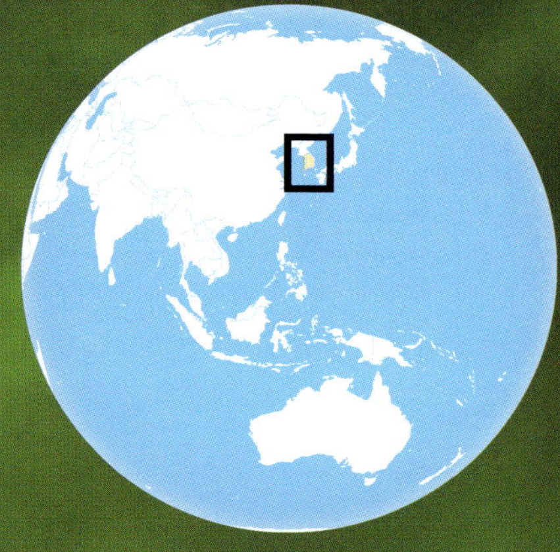

MOUNTAINS AND RIVERS

The name *Korea* stems from *Goryeo* or *Koryo*, the name of an ancient kingdom that first ruled the peninsula in 918 BCE. This name has been translated to mean "high and clear." Other interpretations include "land of high mountains and sparkling streams" and "land of the morning calm." The ancient name is fitting because South Korea is covered in tall mountains and snaking waterways. There are so many mountains on the peninsula that only about one-fifth of the country's land is flat enough to be used for agriculture.[4]

One of the largest mountain ranges in South Korea is the Taebaek Mountains. These mountains extend along the eastern coastline and north into North Korea. The Sobaek Mountains, which switch back and forth in the shape of an S across the peninsula, are just slightly taller than the Taebaeks. The highest point in this mountain range is Mount Jiri, at 6,283 feet (1,915 m) tall.[5]

Rivers and streams in South Korea are important because they supply drinking water for cities and irrigate crops in agricultural areas. They also provide

JIRISAN NATIONAL PARK

Jirisan National Park is one of 22 national parks in South Korea.[6] At 182 square miles (472 sq km), it is the country's oldest and largest national park, stretching across three of South Korea's nine provinces. It's home to Cheonwangbong, the tallest mountain on mainland South Korea.

Visitors who travel to Jirisan can hike 15.8 miles (25.5 km) of trails up and down 13 different peaks.[7] The forests in the national park are covered in Korean winter hazel, cherry, and millennium pine trees. Korean winter hazel trees are known for their pale yellow flowers.

About 1,080 square miles (2,800 sq km) of South Korea's total area is water.[10]

habitats for animals. The country's three major rivers are the Han, Geum, and Nakdong. The Han and Nakdong originate in the Taebaek Mountains. The Geum begins in the southwest.

The Han and Geum flow into the Yellow Sea. The Nakdong River, South Korea's longest river, runs south for 325 miles (523 km) to the Korean Strait.[8] Other major rivers include the Imjin, which flows through North and South Korea and forms an estuary with the Han River; the Bukhan, which flows into the Han; the Yeongsan in the southwest of the country; and the Seomjin, which begins near the head of the Geum and flows into the Korean Strait.

LOWLAND PLAINS

The lowlands make up approximately 30 percent of South Korea's landmass.[9] These areas are situated along the coasts, especially the western and southern coasts, and along the major rivers. The five major lowland areas include the Pyeongtaek coastal plain, located southwest of Seoul; the Geum River basin; the Nakdong River basin; the Han River plain; and the Honam plains, located around the Yeongsan River.

Most of the country's major population centers and fishing villages are situated in these lowland areas because of their relatively flat terrain. In contrast, South Korea's eastern coast has steep cliffs. Except for the far northeastern and southeastern coasts and river valleys, the East Sea coastal plains are relatively unpopulated.

Upo Wetland is a lowland area in southern South Korea formed partially by floodwaters from the Nakdong River. It is an important habitat for many animal species.

Freshwater wetlands are scattered throughout the coastal areas, the lowland plains, and the floodplains of South Korea's three major rivers. Natural wetlands include marshes, swamps, and bogs. They have water-saturated soil or standing water for a large portion of the year. Farmers also create artificial wetlands by flooding human-made rice fields between May and July using surface water from nearby rivers and streams. The fields are harvested in September or October and left dry throughout the winter.

Intertidal flats are areas of the coastline where the shore is alternately exposed and covered by the ebbing and flowing tides. These are found mostly along the western and southern coasts of South Korea, in and adjacent to the Yellow Sea. This region is home to one of the largest tidal flat ecosystems in the world. These brackish, muddy flats are natural habitats for migratory birds, and people also use them for shellfish farming.

VOLCANIC ISLANDS

Off the coast of South Korea, there is a string of more than 3,000 volcanic islands. One of the most famous, and South Korea's largest at 713 square miles (1,846 sq km), is Jeju Island. It is located off the southern coast. Here, high levels of humidity and frequent rainfall give rise to a jungle biome. The highest peak in South Korea is Hallasan mountain, a now-extinct volcano on Jeju. It stands 6,398 feet (1,950 m) above sea level.[11]

Jeju is also home to Geomunoreum, a network of lava tubes and caves. These dark and winding pathways have multicolored carbonate ceilings and floors and charred lava walls.

AN ART PARADISE

At first glance, Jangdo Island resembles an abandoned outcropping off the coast of Yeosu in southern South Korea. But when the tide is low, visitors can cross a bridge from the mainland to access Jangdo's sandy beaches and other natural features. Jangdo is also a showcase for local and international artists. There are murals, sculptures, stone statues, and even a few traditional pagodas along the island's walking paths.

Geomunoreum is interesting and breathtaking to scientists and visitors alike. The lava tubes and caves have been designated a United Nations Educational, Scientific and Cultural Organization (UNESCO) World Natural Heritage site.

Beyond Jeju, many of South Korea's other islands are popular destinations for fishing and tourism. Simnipo Beach is located at the northern tip of Yeongheungdo Island. Marado Island is South Korea's southernmost point. Its rugged coastline is sprinkled with rocky caves flanked by meadows full of flame grass. Jisimdo is an island in the South Sea. Some people call it a floating forest because 37 species of trees grow on the island. The Dokdo Islands, also called Liancort Rocks and Takeshima Islands, are a group of 91 small islands in the Sea of Japan between Japan and South Korea.[12] Because of a historical border dispute, both Japan and South Korea claim the rocky islands as their country's own.

Not all of South Korea's islands receive visitors. Oeyeondo Island is 33 miles (53 km) away from the nearest South Korean port.[13] It is so far from South Korea that folk tales claim island residents can hear roosters crow in China. Seongapdo Island is privately owned, has no ferry access, and isn't accessible to the public. On one side, towering, rocky walls look out toward the sea. On the other, a

Deogyusan Mountain is known for its beauty in winter. The mountain has several hiking trails and a gondola lift that allow visitors to reach its peak even in snowy months.

volcanic crater filled with seawater contains a hidden bay. Seongapdo Island is so mysterious that it was the fictional location for the hit South Korean Netflix series *Squid Game*.

CLIMATE

South Korea is a small country, but its climate is varied. It has four distinct seasons. From December to March, South Korean winters are cold and dry, with an average temperature of about 33 degrees Fahrenheit (0.6°C).[14] There is plenty of snowfall in January for winter sports such as skiing and snowboarding.

From March to May, spring hits South Korea. Temperatures fluctuate during this time. Spring is also the season when yellow dust storms bringing sand from the Gobi Desert and China whip across the country, sometimes for several days at a time.

In summer, from June to August, 60 percent of the country's annual rainfall pummels the region. From late June to late July, the East Asian monsoons bring typhoons, floods, and landslides. It is warm and humid outside, with temperatures hitting more than 90 degrees Fahrenheit (32°C).[15] After such sweltering temperatures, fall brings milder conditions and displays of colorful foliage to South Korea.

Similarly to other places around the world, South Korea is affected by climate change. Average temperatures have risen during all four seasons. Although precipitation has increased, the number of rainy days per month has decreased, meaning that most storms are more intense. Climate change has led to longer summers and shorter winters overall in South Korea.

A WALL OF DUST

For millions of people across northern Asia, dust storms are normal during certain times of year. These *Hwang Sa*, or yellow dust storms, occur every spring in South Korea. High winds in the Gobi Desert between China and Mongolia pick up massive amounts of sand and whisk it across the continent. When this happens, the sky turns yellow and buildings, cars, and people walking outside get covered in a layer of dust. The dust storms can cause people to develop breathing issues, red eyes, and sore throats. Yellow dust storms can last anywhere from a few hours to a few days. In 2023 one storm lasted 24 days total.[16]

CHAPTER **THREE**

PLANTS AND ANIMALS

South Korea is a rocky landmass surrounded on three sides by water. Scientists estimate that there are more than 100,000 plant and animal species that call the forests, wetlands, and coastal plains of South Korea their home.[1] Massive mammals such as the Siberian tiger, South Korea's unofficial national animal, have mostly disappeared over the past few centuries because of poaching, habitat loss, and other factors. But the country is still home to many magnificent creatures.

LUSH FOREST HABITATS

In ancient times, forests covered about two-thirds of what is now South Korea.[2] But over the past 100 years,

Siberian tigers once roamed South Korea. Today, these big cats are found in South Korea only in captivity, such as in zoos.

people cut down many trees to use their wood for construction materials, fuel, and heat. Farmers throughout the vast countryside practiced slash-and-burn agriculture to boost nutrient deposits in the soil because they didn't have access to fertilizer. This involved cutting down vegetation and burning it to create a nutrient-rich, ashy layer for planting crops. After some time, farmers would abandon the charred area and move to a new plot of land to repeat the process. By the end of the Korean War, more than 30 percent of the previously forested land in South Korea had been depleted.[3]

Today, most of these habitats have been replanted, thanks to reforestation efforts. About 63 percent of South Korea is covered in forests.[4] There are three types of forests sprinkled throughout the country: coniferous, deciduous, and areas with a mixture of both coniferous and deciduous trees and shrubs.

South Korea's coniferous forests are full of trees that bear cones and have needlelike leaves that do not all drop at once. The predominant coniferous species are Japanese larch trees, pitch pines, and Korean red pine trees. Korean red pines are found in forests on islands and the mainland. In South

SOUTH KOREA'S REFORESTATION PLAN

Beginning in the 1960s, the South Korean government made a concerted effort to reverse the problem of deforestation. First, it boosted the nation's coal production, reducing the country's reliance on wood for fuel. Then it enlisted the help of elementary school children nationwide to plant hundreds of thousands of trees and hired town residents to tend to the saplings. By the late 1980s, most of the country's bare forests had been replenished. Since 1991, the Korea International Cooperation Agency has helped support similar reforestation efforts in China, Mongolia, Myanmar, and Indonesia.

The Korean fir tree is native to South Korea. This species is known for its purplish seed cones.

Korea's southern region and on Jeju Island, bay laurel trees are common. They become twisted and gnarled as they get exposed to salty coastal gales.

Deciduous trees have leaves that change color and drop in autumn before regrowing in spring. In South Korea's deciduous broad-leaved forests, trees such as maples and birches thrive. Here, towering Mongolian oaks, sawtooth oaks, Oriental cork oaks, and Jolcham oaks grow at high altitudes in the middle and southern regions, including on many of South Korea's mountains. Other species in these deciduous forests include black locust trees, East Asian alders, and blossoming Sargent's cherry trees. In late spring and early summer, the white and slightly fragrant, bell-shaped flowers of snowbell trees hang from outstretched branches full of dark green foliage.

There are about 5,350 known plant species in South Korea.[5]

Hidden throughout South Korea's forests, there are also a number of rare or endangered trees and other plants. Some of these are included on the Korean Red List of Threatened Species. This list provides scientific data to inform government decisions about which species to protect.

Athyrium spinulosum is a green fern that's found only in the Samcheok and Inje areas in Gangwon-do. It grows along the forested peaks of mountains near hiking trails. *Gymnadenia conopsea* is a purple-flowered herb that sprouts in Gyeonggi-do and Jeju-do. It lives amid the sunny grasslands of tall mountains. *Iris ruthenica* is a vibrant purple flowering plant. It grows in grasslands, lowland forests, and sandy areas in Gangwon-do, Gyeonggi-do, and Cheongchungnam-do. It provides a feeding ground for insects.

ANIMALS BIG AND SMALL

South Korea is known for its packed urban areas, where the only living creatures around aside from insects and birds are domesticated dogs and cats. Beyond its crowded metropolises, the country is home to unique wildlife. Many of its larger land and sea predators have vanished over the past few hundred years. Sea lions, for example, were a regular presence on Dokdo Island centuries ago. But aggressive hunting by the Japanese during their occupation of South Korea in the early 1900s eliminated the sea lion population.

A WILDLIFE SANCTUARY

The demilitarized zone (DMZ) is a strip of land between North and South Korea that is no longer populated by humans. Once a vast area of fertile farmland, it is now a refuge for wildlife. Approximately 6,170 species of plants and animals live in the DMZ.[6] These include lynxes, long-tailed mountain goats, musk deer, Mongolian racerunners, Manchurian trout, golden eagles, and yellow-throated martens. Once a symbol of prosperity and peace, the red-crowned cranes found drinking from streams in this region are one of the rarest crane species in the world.

Siberian tigers no longer roam the dense forests of the Korean Peninsula. Humans destroyed their habitats by building towns and roads. Siberian tigers have been nearly eliminated from Asia. They now live only in a few protected wildlife reserves. Still, other animals thrive in South Korea.

Many species live in the country's national parks. Bukhansan is a national park adjacent to Seoul. The park is littered with wild boars that have adapted to human presence. They crash through the underbrush and forage for food scraps left behind by park visitors. The South Korean government has designated these nocturnal, bristly

Male Siberian musk deer have long canine teeth that continue to grow for their entire lives.

animals as harmful to farmland and grazing areas in parks and has been controlling their population size.

Seoraksan National Park in the northeastern province of Gangwon provides the perfect home for otters, which scurry and slide through mountain streams and wetland areas. Flying squirrels whiz through the air. Siberian musk deer throughout this region hide from predators by burrowing through tiny openings in the rocky outcroppings. Due to their small stature and sturdy legs, these deer can run extraordinarily fast.

Korean gorals, a species of wild goat, have short necks, stubby legs, pointed horns, and rough hooves that allow them to climb up and down craggy terrain. Over time, they have adapted to live in caves that other animals cannot access. Korean gorals travel in small groups to find food.

The Asiatic black bear, also called a moon bear because of the light-colored, moon-shaped marking on its glossy black chest, is native to South Korea's forests. It dines on insects, birds, small mammals, honey, and fruits and nuts that grow throughout the wooded areas. Asiatic black bears can live up to 25 years in the wild.[7] Because these bears are expert climbers, they will clamber up trees to find food, sunbathe, nap, and hide from predators. In the winter, their fur grows thicker to protect them from the cold. Asiatic black bears are among the largest tree-dwelling mammals in the world.

REPTILES AND INSECTS

Plenty of insects and reptiles, such as spiders, snakes, mosquitoes, and beetles, fly, crawl, and slither throughout South Korea. One species is the yellow-bellied sea snake, which is found in seas surrounding the country. With a bright-yellow underside and slick black top, this dangerous reptile carries a strong toxin in its fangs. For people, just one small bite from a yellow-bellied sea snake can cause muscle pain, stiffness, extreme tiredness, and vomiting. In very rare cases, a bite from this snake can lead to paralysis and death.

The Asian giant hornet lives throughout Asia, including in South Korea. Also called a murder hornet, this flying bug is the largest hornet in the world, measuring up to two inches (5 cm) in length.[8] It has a large yellow-orange head, a black-and-orange striped belly, and a painful, venomous sting. Although humans can die if stung by an Asian giant hornet, the insect's main target is honeybees. The hornet often kills an entire hive in just a few hours.

The yellow-bellied sea snake has a spotted, paddle-like tail. The tail's shape helps the snake swim.

Not all reptiles and insects in South Korea are toxic or deadly. The Asian comma is a black-and-yellow spotted butterfly with a white, comma-shaped marking on its wings. It has a wingspan of about 2.3 inches (5.8 cm) and camouflages itself in the leaves of trees and other plants to hide from predators.[9]

BIRDS

Migratory birds find habitats throughout South Korea. Of the 62 species of herons found around the world, 18 of them live in the southern part of the Korean Peninsula.[10] Black-crowned night herons, Chinese pond herons, cattle egrets, Pacific reef egrets, and Chinese egrets breed in flocks around low, hilly forests near villages or in the wooded areas of uninhabited islands. They eat small fish, crustaceans, insects, lizards, and mollusks found in watery areas or streams.

Various species of cranes live in wetlands or grasslands along South Korea's coasts. For some cranes, South Korea is a temporary home. Seven species of cranes fly through or spend the winter in South Korea, migrating away from colder temperatures to the north. These species include the red-crowned crane, white-naped crane, hooded crane, Eurasian crane, sandhill crane, Siberian crane, and demoiselle crane. South Korea's tidal flats along the Yellow Sea serve as a stopover point for 50 million shorebirds as they travel 18,000 miles (28,968 km) from eastern Russia and Alaska in the summer to Australia and New Zealand in the winter.[11]

SEA CREATURES

Dozens of species of sea creatures swim in the water or bask on South Korea's rocky shores. Intertidal flats are areas rich in biodiversity. Many types of crustacean, fish, and plankton populations do well in this environment. These creatures serve as food for migratory birds and mammals that live in the open waters. The finless porpoise and spotted seal live in the seas bordering the southern part of the country, including in the rugged inlets off the coast of Jeollanam-do and Gyeongsangnam-do. South Korea is also a stopping ground for migrating whales.

In recent years, South Korean fishers have been criticized for capturing dolphins and beluga whales for use in live aquarium shows. Bibongi, the last endangered Indo-Pacific bottlenose dolphin held in captivity in South Korea, was returned to the wild in 2022 after 17 years performing at a marine park on Jeju Island.[12] Commercial whaling is not legal in South Korea. However, these laws are not strictly enforced, and there are loopholes for fishers who accidentally catch whales in fish nets. Many fishers claim to accidentally catch minke whales, which are then processed for meat.

Many types of turtles are found throughout the country too. One of the best places to see migrating sea turtles in South Korea is off the coast and on the sandy shores of Jeju Island. Green, loggerhead, hawksbill, olive ridley, and leatherback turtles all stop here to rest, find food, mate, lay eggs, and nest at different times throughout the year.

SOUTH KOREA'S NATIONAL BIRD

In 1964 the South Korean government staged a contest to pick a national bird. The magpie won in a landslide. Magpies are black-and-white birds, usually about 18 inches (45 cm) long.[13] They live throughout South Korea in the mountains, coastal plains, and villages. In Korean mythology, magpies formed a bridge to help two star-crossed lovers reunite. They are also seen as messengers of happy news and good fortune. In 1996 magpies were taken off the list of birds that could be hunted as game fowl in South Korea.

Gray whales swim near Ulsan, South Korea, each year as they migrate south. Their path near South Korea is designated as a natural monument to protect the endangered species.

CHAPTER **FOUR**

HISTORY

South Korea has a history full of periods of growth and positive change accompanied by periods of violence, war, and strife. Approximately 700,000 years ago, people first started migrating to the Korean Peninsula from Manchuria and Siberia. They settled in small communities centered in the present-day provinces of Pyeongannam-do, Gyeonggi-do, and Chungcheongnam-do. These first peoples survived by living in caves, hunting animals, and foraging for edible plants.

Over thousands of years, different regimes rose and began to reign over the peninsula. This period culminated in the Joseon dynasty, which lasted from 1392 to 1910 and was led by a series of kings. Throughout this dynasty, the peninsula was invaded by warring outsiders, including Japan in 1592 and

Yi Seong-gye became King Taejo in 1392 when he took the throne as the first ruler during the Joseon dynasty.

In 1945 many Koreans welcomed US Army forces who had arrived to help liberate the nation from Japanese occupation.

the Manchu tribes of Manchuria in 1627. By the mid-1600s, Korea's leaders decided to close their borders to the outside world in order to limit invasions. During this time, the country experienced an unprecedented period of peace with its neighbors. However, it faced internal political turmoil and weakening leadership as social unrest inside the country grew.

This isolationist time lasted until the 1870s, when Japan approached Korea to resume international relations. Countries such as China, the United States, and Britain followed suit and forged new trade relationships with Korea. By the beginning of the 1900s, Japan, Russia, and China had begun fighting for overall control of the region. In 1904 a full-blown war between Russia and Japan ignited, culminating in a Japanese victory on September 5, 1905. Japan occupied Korea and overthrew its government. Five years later, Korea was formally annexed by Japan.

For 35 years, the Korean people were treated brutally by Japanese leaders. Koreans could not speak out against their Japanese rulers. Korean history and the Korean language were no longer taught in schools. The Japanese confiscated Korean farmers' land, and many Korean-owned businesses were forced to close. Some Koreans were required to change their names to ones that sounded more Japanese. During World War II (1939–1945), many Korean men were made to serve in Japan's army and work many grueling hours in wartime factories. Thousands of Korean women were sexually abused by Japanese soldiers.

A DIVIDED KOREA

At the end of World War II, the Axis powers, including Japan, lost to the Allies, a military coalition of countries including the United States, the United Kingdom (previously called Britain), the Soviet Union, and China. In 1945 the Soviet Union and the United States divided Korea into two temporarily separate entities to oversee the peaceful removal of Japanese forces from the Korean Peninsula. The area north of latitude 38 degrees north, a line also called the thirty-eighth parallel, was overseen by the Soviet Union, a communist country in which the government controlled everything and people shared the wealth they created. In the south, an interim military government was installed by the United States, a democratic country in which the people had the power to make decisions directly or through elected representatives.

Although the Allies' initial intention was to let the Koreans eventually unify and determine their own future, neither the United States nor the Soviet Union wanted to see the other's political influences win out in the region. Consequently, in 1948, the temporary division between North and South Korea became permanent, with pro-communist influences in the north and pro-democratic influences in the south.

The Soviet Union installed Kim Il-sung as the first president of the Democratic People's Republic of Korea, or North Korea. In the southern part of the Korean Peninsula, anti-communist leader Syngman Rhee was chosen as president of the Republic of Korea (ROK) by the country's legislative body, the National Assembly. Rhee was backed by the United States. Seoul became South Korea's capital. On July 17, 1948, the nation's first constitution was adopted.

THE DOMINO THEORY

After World War II, a major part of US foreign policy was guided by anti-communist beliefs. The US strategy had to do with what President Harry S. Truman called the domino theory. In this hypothetical situation, the fall of one country to communism would inevitably lead to a chain reaction of other countries falling to communist aggressors around the world. The threat of South Korea falling into communist hands was one of the chief reasons the United States supported South Korea and fought for its independence as a democratic country.

South Korea's constitution has been amended nine times since its adoption in 1948.[3]

During the next two years, border disputes between North Korea and South Korea were widespread and deadly. Nearly 10,000 North Korean and South Korean soldiers were killed in these fights.[1] On June 25, 1950, the Korean People's Army, backed by the Soviet Union and eventually China, invaded South Korea in an attempt to reunify the country under communist rule. This was the beginning of the Korean War.

With the help of air, naval, and ground forces from the United States and other members of the United Nations (UN), South Korea defended its independence for three years. By the time the Korean War ended in 1953, more than 137,000 South Korean and 520,000 North Korean soldiers had been killed. Nearly 245,000 South Korean civilians and 282,000 North Korean civilians had died as well.[2]

The UN command, North Korea, and China signed an armistice agreement on July 27, 1953. President Rhee abstained from signing the agreement because he wanted to settle the unification issue through a more formal and final end-of-war peace treaty. The armistice was technically a temporary agreement, but it marked the end of the Korean War and was never replaced by a permanent peace agreement. The armistice specified that the border between North and South Korea would remain in about the same place where it had been before the war. To separate the two countries, an unpopulated corridor called the demilitarized zone (DMZ) was created along the border.

Park Chung-hee, *center*, is known as South Korea's most influential leader during the 1900s.

MILITARY RULE

After the Korean War ended in 1953, South Korea was an independent republic. The country stayed in a fragile state for more than three decades. During much of that time, the government was controlled by a series of militant rulers.

Rhee remained in office as president until 1960, when a series of popular uprisings and student demonstrations over supposed election fraud forced him to resign. A new parliamentary government led by Prime Minister Chang Myon emerged. This new government marked the beginning of South Korea's Second Republic.

Then in a military coup on May 16, 1961, General Park Chung-hee dissolved the National Assembly and took over. In October 1963, he officially became president of South Korea's Third Republic and ruled with an iron fist. Throughout the 1960s and 1970s under Park's reign, South Korea advanced economically. It became one of the fastest-growing economies in the world. But that progress came at a cost. Although South Korea remained a democracy on the surface, people there did not have all the freedoms that their government promised.

Park's government maintained strict control over the press, the judicial system, and colleges and universities. He expanded the Korean Central Intelligence Agency (KCIA), a group officially in charge of maintaining order but unofficially responsible for repressing people politically. In 1972 he dissolved the legislature once again and installed a new authoritarian regime with an amended constitution that left no room for dissenters. For the next six years, anti-government riots broke out all over the country and were suppressed by government troops.

In 1979 Park was assassinated and a new, even more repressive military government formed under General Chun Doo-hwan. Two years later, the constitution was amended, establishing the Fifth Republic. By 1987 South Koreans were still deeply dissatisfied with Chun's oppressive government. That year, Chun was forced out of office because of

THE GWANGJU UPRISING

Gwangju is a city in southwestern South Korea. An uprising in the city led to one of the most brutal responses in the country's history. Between May 18 and 27, 1980, hundreds of thousands of South Koreans, many of them students, participated in protests against what they considered to be an oppressive military regime that restricted their personal freedom.[4] In response and backed by the United States, General Chun Doo-hwan sent tanks, ground forces, and helicopters from the ROK Airborne Brigade to quash the demonstrations. Hundreds of people died, and thousands were injured.[5]

civil unrest and mounting international pressure. The constitution was amended again. It allowed the direct election of a president for the first time.

AN ERA OF DEMOCRACY

In 1987 South Korea held the first free elections in its short history. Former army general Roh Tae-woo was elected to office in a direct vote by the people. He ran on a platform that aimed to curb government corruption and bring democracy to the people through a series of reforms. He also tried to restore relations with former international enemies, including the Soviet Union, China, Hungary, Poland, and Yugoslavia.

In February 1993, Kim Young-sam, South Korea's first civilian president in more than 30 years, succeeded Roh Tae-woo. He ushered in more reforms, including firing hundreds of unethical bureaucrats and military leaders, releasing thousands of political leaders who had been imprisoned during the long military reign over the country, and launching a major anti-corruption initiative in government and economic offices. During the 1980s and into the 1990s, the technology sector blossomed in South Korea, advancing the country's image throughout the world.

South Korea's next few presidents continued the country's progression toward true democracy. President Kim Dae-jung won the Nobel Peace Prize in 2000 for trying to initiate a truce with still-communist North Korea. In 2013 Park Chung-hee's daughter, Park Geun-hye, became the first woman to be elected leader of South Korea.

PRESENT-DAY SOUTH KOREA

Between the end of the Korean War and the 2000s, South Korea's population more than doubled. In 2024 there were nearly ten million people in Seoul alone.[6] Since its birth as an independent nation, South Korea has gone through immense changes in all aspects of society. Today it is a democracy that mostly respects the rights of its people.

Since the turn of the millennium, South Korea has experienced many advancements as well as setbacks. For one, relations with North Korea remain at a standstill. North Korean aggression and nuclear tests have affected inter-Korean relations. In April 2018, leaders of North and South Korea met for a summit for the first time in more than ten years. At the conclusion of these talks, South Korean president Moon Jae-in and North Korea's Kim Jong-un signed a joint declaration pledging to work toward reducing nuclear arms on the Korean Peninsula.

The COVID-19 pandemic spread around the world in early 2020. The South Korean government

SOUTH KOREA HOSTS THE OLYMPICS

South Korea has experienced great political strife throughout its history. But it has also achieved cultural milestones. In 1988 Seoul hosted the Summer Olympics. A new sports complex was constructed to host athletes from across the globe. The subway system was expanded. Brand-new highways in and out of the city were built. This infrastructure still serves South Koreans today. In 2018 the Olympic Games were once again hosted by South Korea. This time the Winter Olympic Games were held in Pyeongchang, located in the Taebaek Mountains.

During Yoon's brief martial law declaration in 2024, certain activities, including meetings of the National Assembly, were prohibited. Armed soldiers entered the Assembly building.

enacted strict public health measures to limit the spread of the disease. These actions were authorized through the Infectious Diseases Control and Prevention Act, which allows the executive branch to impose quarantines, monitor the public, and collect personal data. Though many experts saw the country's response as especially effective, others saw the government's collection and disclosure of citizens' location information and health data as violating basic human rights.

In 2022 Yoon Suk-yeol of the conservative People's Power Party won the presidential election in South Korea. On the seventy-seventh anniversary of the day South Korea became independent, he gave a speech touting his intention to keep peace talks with North Korea open. "Denuclearization of North Korea is essential for sustainable peace on the Korean Peninsula, in Northeast Asia and around the world," he said.[7]

But in 2024 the relationship between the two countries soured once more. North Korean leaders said they were ceasing all economic cooperation with South Korea. They called South Korea the "principal enemy" of North Korea and destroyed two roads along the border with their southern neighbor.[8] In response, South Korea strengthened its military presence within the area.

On December 3, 2024, President Yoon Suk-yeol declared martial law in South Korea. He claimed this was necessary to protect the country from North Korean forces. However, many experts believe Yoon was trying to seize power from the opposition-led National Assembly. According to the nation's constitution, martial law grants the president extraordinary power to preserve order during states of emergency. Within hours the National Assembly voted to end martial law, declaring Yoon's actions unconstitutional. Yoon faced calls for impeachment.

CHAPTER **FIVE**

PEOPLE AND CULTURE

South Korea is full of densely populated cities, bustling ports, and rich cultural traditions. Its population is about 52 million, with approximately equal numbers of women and men. In 2024 the country had the fifteenth-highest life expectancy in the world.[1]

In 2023 about 81 percent of people in South Korea lived in cities.[2] The country is mostly ethnically homogeneous. Approximately 96 percent of the people who live there are Korean.[3]

South Korean culture adheres to traditional gender roles in regard to sexual identity and dating. Most people, especially those in older generations, consider someone's gender to be binary (male or female) and

BLACKPINK is a female K-pop group that has worked to push back on restrictive gender norms in South Korea's music industry. The group's songs are confident and empowering.

determined by their biological sex at birth. A person identifying with another gender has no legal way to redefine their gender on identifying documents, such as their birth certificate, driver's license, or passport. Many people who identify as LGBTQ stay very discreet. Same-sex marriage or other forms of legal partnership are not allowed.

LANGUAGE

Korean is the official language of South Korea. It is spoken by more than 75 million people around the world.[4] The language is written and spoken slightly differently in North and South Korea.

Hangul is the writing system of the Korean language. Its alphabet has 24 letters, including 14 consonants and ten vowels. Hangul was created in the 1400s by King Sejong the Great because he believed the Chinese alphabet Koreans were using at the time was too complicated. In Hangul, the shapes of the consonants are based on the shape the mouth makes when speaking the sound of the letter. The shapes of the vowels are based on three elements: humanity (a vertical line), Earth (a horizontal line), and heaven (a dot).

South Korea has 16 UNESCO World Heritage sites, including 14 cultural sites and two natural ones.[5]

Hangul is a phonemic alphabet, meaning it is written the same way it sounds. Each letter represents a specific sound, and each sound can change depending on the context of the word or the rules of the language. Words are made of letters that are grouped into syllabic blocks that have an initial consonant, one or two vowels, and sometimes a consonant at the end. Until the 1980s, Korean was usually written from right to left in vertical columns. Over the last few decades, writing from left to right in horizontal lines has risen in popularity. Today, the majority of texts are written in this way.

A PLACE OF CALM

Bongeunsa Temple is a sacred Buddhist site in the heart of Seoul that was built in 794 BCE. Originally named Gyeonseongsa, it was relocated to its current spot during the reign of Myeongjong in the mid-1500s CE. The temple is seen as a symbol of the revival of Buddhism throughout South Korea. It contains more than 3,400 Buddhist scriptures and a replica of Maitreya, the Future Buddha, that stands 91 feet (28 m) tall.[6] This is one of the tallest stone statues in the country. Two drum ceremonies are held on the grounds each day.

RELIGION

South Korea's culture is steeped in deep spiritual beliefs. The main religions practiced in South Korea are Protestantism and Buddhism. A small group of South Koreans practice Catholicism. The country is one of the only places in the world where both Christmas and Buddha's Birthday are celebrated as public holidays. Buddha's Birthday falls on the eighth day of the lunar calendar's fourth month. This festival honors the birth of the Buddha, who founded Buddhism in about the 400s BCE. It also celebrates Korean culture.

Other spiritual practices that exist in South Korea include Won Buddhism, Confucianism, Islam, and Shamanism. Shamanism is the only indigenous religion practiced in the country. In 2023, 63 percent

In 2021, 17 percent of South Koreans identified as Protestants, 16 percent identified as Buddhists, 6 percent identified as Catholics, and the rest didn't adhere to any one religion.[8]

of South Koreans said they were not religious or didn't identify with any particular religion.[7]

Architecturally, some of the most ornate and sacred buildings in South Korea are dedicated to religious practice. Haedong Younggungsa is a Buddhist temple in Busan. Perched above a rocky cliff looking out into the sea, the structure was originally built in 1376. In front of its main sanctuary is a three-story pagoda with four lions. The animals symbolize joy, anger, sadness, and happiness. The Myeong-dong Cathedral is the church for the Archdiocese of Seoul and was also the birthplace of the Roman Catholic community in Korea. A stone-and-brick building with a clock tower and towering stained-glass windows, it houses the remains of honored saints.

FOOD AND DRINK

Korean food is full of unique flavors and colorful ingredients. A typical Korean meal is made of a bowl of rice, a bowl of soup or stew, and a few side dishes. Often some sort of protein, such as seafood, beef, chicken, pork, or tofu, is showcased in the meal along with plenty of vegetables.

Some of the most popular dishes include bibimbap (a stir-fry in a sizzling clay pot), *mandoo* (Korean dumplings), bulgogi (marinated beef), and soups such as *seolleongtang* (Korean ox bone soup). Similarly to those in other East Asian countries, many of these dishes include soy sauce, garlic, and ginger as flavor enhancers. South Koreans also use two other key ingredients

Several Buddhist temples in South Korea decorate with paper lanterns to celebrate Buddha's Birthday.

when cooking to make their dishes uniquely Korean: gochujang, which is fermented chili paste, and *doenjang,* fermented soybean paste.

Korean meals are often eaten family style. At home or in restaurants, groups of diners order a multitude of dishes to be shared among everyone sitting at the table. One of the most popular

When people eat Korean barbecue, they need to cook each slice of meat for only a few minutes.

family-style dining experiences is Korean barbecue. A plate of raw beef is delivered to the table, which has a grill in the center. Diners take turns grilling the meat. Then they add accompaniments from the *banchan*, or small plates placed around the table. Some popular banchan dishes include kimchi, sweet and crunchy radish salad, spicy cucumber salad, and shredded squid sautéed in sesame oil and garlic.

To accompany a meal or just as a snack, there are plenty of beverages to enjoy that are uniquely Korean. *Misutgaru* is similar to a protein shake. It is made with grains, nuts, ice, and a sweetening ingredient such as honey. *Sikye* is a sweet rice drink that's often served as dessert. *Milkis* is a carbonated Korean soda that combines milk and corn syrup. Korean tea is made from edible plants, including chrysanthemum, green plum, and yuzu.

KIMJANG

Kimchi is a spicy dish of fermented vegetables, often featuring cabbage. It is the unofficial national dish of South Korea. But it is also part of a cultural tradition called *kimjang*. For centuries, people all over South Korea have gathered to practice the art of making kimchi. Over the course of a few days every November, South Korean neighbors still get together to preserve pounds of napa cabbage by salting the leaves, mixing them with peppery sauce, and preserving them in jars so they can be enjoyed throughout the year. In 2013 UNESCO designated kimjang as a marker of national cultural heritage.

HALLYU!

South Korea is known for all types of ancient artistic traditions, including pottery, folk dancing, theater, calligraphy, and mural painting of Buddhist deities. But in recent years, the modern artistic movement of *hallyu*, translated as "the Korean wave," has exploded across the world. Perhaps one of the artistic fields South Korea is best known for is music, especially K-pop, the genre that first took the world by storm in the 2010s.

Rapper Psy was the one of the biggest breakout K-pop stars to emerge on the international stage. His 2012 satirical hit "Gangnam Style" topped the charts thanks to its music video, which went viral. It was the first YouTube video to be viewed one billion times.[9] Boy band BTS, producing a mix of hip-hop and electronica, also became a massive success. In May 2018, BTS became the first K-pop group to debut at number one on the US *Billboard* 200 album chart.[10]

Another area in which South Koreans excel is movies and television. Beginning in the mid-1990s and continuing into the 2000s, South Korean TV dramas and movies were some of the most popular forms of entertainment watched by people worldwide. *Dae Jang Geum*, a TV historical drama about royal cuisine, aired between 2003 and 2004. It was shown in 91 countries around the world. In 2020 the film *Parasite* won four major awards at the

BUCHAECHUM, THE FAN DANCE

Buchaechum, also called the Fan Dance, is a Korean shamanic ritual dance that was traditionally performed by a group of dancers using large leaves to ward off evil spirits. Today, the choreographed dance is performed using fans decorated with brightly colored peonies and feathers. The dancers, usually women, move into formations that resemble images of flowers in bloom, birds in flight, waves crashing, or butterflies flapping their wings. The dancers wear lavishly decorated hanbok and jewelry. Most of the time, the dancing is accompanied by traditional Korean folk songs.

BTS became a global cultural phenomenon, bringing more attention to South Korean language, culture, and food.

MINI **BIO**

HOYEON

Hoyeon, born Jung Ho-yeon, was a star of Netflix's hit TV show *Squid Game* in 2021. In 2022 she won a Screen Actors Guild Award for her role as Kang Sae-byeok in the series' first season. This was Hoyeon's first acting role.

Born in Seoul in 1994, Hoyeon always wanted to be a supermodel. She began modeling in 2010 and participated in Seoul Fashion Week as a teenager. Two years later, she got a modeling agent, and in 2013 she was the runner-up in the competitive reality TV show *Korea's Next Top Model*. Hoyeon went on to have an international modeling career, representing brands such as Chanel, Burberry, and Gucci.

Today, Hoyeon's career has blossomed far beyond *Squid Game*. In 2024 she starred opposite Cate Blanchett in the Apple TV+ series *Disclaimer*. She is also a global ambassador for the brands Louis Vuitton, Adidas, and Lancôme.

In addition to representing high-end fashion brands in ad campaigns, Hoyeon has modeled in runway shows.

ninety-second Academy Awards, becoming the first foreign language film to win Best Picture.[11] Its awards also included Best International Feature Film, Best Original Screenplay, and Best Director. In the first 28 days after its September 2021 premiere, *Squid Game* became Netflix's most popular series ever. This drama depicts a fictional competition where hundreds of desperate people play a series of children's games with deadly stakes for the chance to win a huge amount of money.

SPORTS AND RECREATION

South Korea is famous for sports as well as art. As in many countries, watching baseball is a beloved pastime. Some of the country's most popular sporting events are Korean Baseball Organization games. Soccer is well liked too. Founded in 1983, the K League is Asia's oldest professional soccer league. Korea's national soccer team has qualified for every men's World Cup since 1986.

The most traditionally Korean sport is tae kwon do. This martial art was created in Korea thousands of years ago. It involves a series of poses and movements including kicking, punching, blocking, dodging, jumping, and sparring that calm the mind and strengthen the body. It is one of the most-practiced martial arts in the world, with more than 80 million people performing it worldwide.[12]

CHAPTER **SIX**

POLITICS

On May 31, 1948, in South Korea's first general election, 198 members of the National Assembly were sworn into office, forming the country's main governing body. On July 17 that year, the country's first constitution was signed into law. One month later, on August 15, South Korea's first form of government officially began.

To commemorate this grand occasion, South Korea adopted its national anthem, a song called "Aegukga," which translates to "Patriotic Song." This anthem celebrates the country's mountainous landscape and resilient people. In English, the song's last verse is "With this spirit and this mind, give all loyalty, in suffering or in joy, to the love of country."[1]

Today, although significant amendments have been made over the years, South Korea's original constitution

The first election in South Korea occurred under tense conditions. Several militant groups threatened citizens with violence in an attempt to sway the election in their own favor.

still stands. Above all, the South Korean Constitution outlines that the nation is a liberal democracy, which means that the power of the central government is limited and that the freedom and rights of individuals are protected by law. It says that South Koreans are entitled to equal political, economic, social, and cultural opportunities regardless of their class status. And it mandates that all people living in the country must pay taxes, serve in the military when qualified, educate their children, and work to support themselves.

South Korea's government consists of three branches. The legislative branch drafts and passes the country's laws. The executive branch enforces the laws and keeps the government running smoothly. The judicial branch interprets the laws, settles disputes, and decides whether certain laws violate the country's constitution.

LEGISLATIVE

South Korea's legislative body, the National Assembly, is in Seoul. It makes all the country's laws. All National Assembly members serve four-year terms.

THE TAEGEUKGI

South Korea's national flag, called the *Taegeukgi*, has a white background that represents brightness, purity, and peace. In the center of the flag is a *taegeuk*, which is a circle with a wavy line in the middle. It symbolizes the harmony between negative cosmic forces (yin, rendered in blue) and positive cosmic forces (yang, rendered in red). Located around the taegeuk are four black-striped graphics. One, called the *geon*, symbolizes the sky. The other three graphics represent earth, water, and fire. As a whole, the flag is a symbol of unity and continual progress for the South Korean people.

SAFE AND FAIR ELECTIONS

In South Korea, there is an independent organization unaffiliated with any political party that has the job of ensuring that all national and local elections are free and fair. Called for in the constitution, the National Election Commission manages funds collected during campaigns, handles election law violations, and keeps track of political party registrations. Members are prohibited from joining a political party or participating in any political activities. Members serve terms of six years.

Since its first session in 1948, the number of seats in the National Assembly has changed over time. In 2024 the National Assembly consisted of 300 seats. Of those, 254 members were directly elected by the people in a majority-wins vote.[2] This means eligible South Korean citizens voted for one candidate in their local constituency, and the candidate with the most votes was elected to the National Assembly.

The remaining 46 members of the National Assembly were elected by a semi-mixed-member proportional representation vote. In this type of electoral system, political parties gain seats in proportion to the number of party votes cast for them. In 2024 South Korean voters were given two ballots: one for district candidates and the other for party preference. After seats were allocated to the winning candidates in each district, remaining seats in the National Assembly were filled based on the party vote. This new system was enacted in 2019 to give popular smaller parties a chance to increase their representation in the legislature, even if their members couldn't win electoral seats in head-to-head races.

Like many countries around the world, South Korea has a multiparty political system. Two parties usually dominate the nation's elections. On April 10, 2024, the twenty-second general

Overall voter turnout for South Korea's 2024 general election was the highest for a general election in 32 years at 67 percent.[5]

election for the National Assembly took place. The liberal-leaning Democratic Party (DP), which supports greater human rights, improved relations with North Korea, and a progressive economic policy, earned a slim majority over the People's Power Party (PPP). The PPP is a more conservative party with policies such as strengthening national defense and upholding traditional family values. The DP took 175 of the 300 seats, the PPP won 108 seats, and the remaining 17 seats went to smaller minority parties.[3]

EXECUTIVE

South Korea's executive branch is organized similarly to the executive branch in the United States. At the top is the president, who is the head of state and leader of the armed forces. Under South Korea's constitution, the president is elected by popular vote. The president serves a single five-year term and cannot be reelected. This prevents any one leader from having too much influence over a long period of time.

In the 2022 presidential election, PPP candidate Yoon Suk-yeol was voted in as South Korea's president by a slim margin. He received 48.6 percent of the vote. Approximately 77 percent of eligible South Korean voters cast ballots in the 2022 presidential election.[4]

Below the president is the State Council, sometimes called the Cabinet. It usually consists of between 15 and 30 members and is led by the president. The prime minister, who is appointed

MINI **BIO**

MOON JAE-IN

Moon Jae-in was born in a refugee center in South Korea in 1953. His parents had fled from North Korea in 1950. While attending law school, Moon became involved in the movement against Park Chung-hee's authoritarian rule. Moon was expelled for his activism and briefly imprisoned, but he eventually completed his degree. He maintained his commitment to democracy throughout his early career as a lawyer, specializing in civil and human rights.

From 2003 to 2007, Moon held the role of senior secretary for civil affairs. He won a seat in the National Assembly in 2012, where he served one term. In 2017, after President Park Geun-hye was impeached, Moon won the presidency in the next election.

Moon was known for his nuanced approach to relations with North Korea. He said, "I am a believer in dialogue, but I also know that dialogue is possible when we have a strong national defense."[6] When the COVID-19 pandemic hit South Korea in 2020, Moon and his administration helped curb the growing number of cases. His public health initiatives increased his popularity through the end of his presidency in 2022.

Moon Jae-in was a member of the Democratic Party. He was South Korea's first liberal president in nearly ten years.

by the president and approved by the National Assembly, is the second-in-command. The prime minister attends meetings of the National Assembly and has the power to weigh in on major national policies. They also manage all the committees and ministries, which are departments in the government that handle specific tasks and are led by members of the Cabinet. If the office of the presidency is vacant or the president is unable to perform their duties for any reason, the prime minister takes over and runs the government.

Members of South Korea's Cabinet are recommended by the prime minister and appointed by the president. They help the president with all sorts of tasks. Their responsibilities include weighing in on declarations of war, providing advice on foreign policy, drafting amendments to the constitution, and setting government budgets.

JUDICIAL

The judicial branch in South Korea consists of the Supreme Court, three appellate courts, district courts, family courts, administrative courts, and a patent court. The Supreme Court is the highest of these. Among other duties, it interprets the constitution and all other South Korean laws, hears appeals against the judgments or rulings of lower courts, and reviews the legality of government activities and regulations.

At the head of the Supreme Court is the chief justice, who is appointed by the president and approved by the National Assembly. The chief justice serves a six-year term. The mandatory retirement age for this job is 70. The other 13 Supreme Court justices are also appointed by the

The Constitutional Court hears cases about impeachment. In 2017 the court unanimously voted to remove President Park Geun-hye from office, a first for the country.

president after being recommended by the chief justice. They serve six-year terms and can serve multiple times. Their mandatory retirement age is 65.

INDEPENDENT GOVERNMENT ORGANIZATIONS

In other areas of South Korea's government, there are different independent organizations that make sure the country's three branches of government are operating in a legal, efficient, and effective manner. One such group, the Constitutional Court of Korea, ensures that the government is adhering to the laws set forth in the constitution. For example, it offers the final decision on impeachment hearings and decides when and how political parties should be dissolved. Nine justices serve on this court. Three are appointed by the president, three are appointed by the Supreme Court chief justice, and three are elected by the National Assembly.

Sejong was established in 2007 to host some of South Korea's government operations because Seoul was becoming crowded. Several national ministries now operate there.

The National Human Rights Commission of Korea (NHRCK) is another government agency. Founded in November 2001, its main goals are to protect, advocate for, and promote essential human rights. Since its launch, the NHRCK has considered petitions, published papers, and worked on cases concerning a variety of issues, including abortion rights, gender recognition for transgender people, and migrant workers' rights.

LOCAL GOVERNMENT

South Korea has many local governments, including those of provinces and metropolises. Provinces are large administrative regions that encompass a wide geographical area, and metropolises are large urban centers within a particular province. There are nine provinces in

South Korea: Jeju, North Jeolla, South Jeolla, North Chungcheong, South Chungcheong, Gangwon, Gyeonggi, North Gyeongsang, and South Gyeongsang. There are eight major metropolises: Busan, Daegu, Incheon, Gwangju, Daejeon, Ulsan, Seoul, and Sejong. Seoul is South Korea's largest city and its capital. It stands on its own and doesn't belong to a province. Sejong is a self-governing city. It is South Korea's administrative capital and is where many official government offices are located.

In each province and metropolis, the local government has a legislative council whose elected members can serve unlimited terms. Below that, there are other lower-level government offices. The provinces are further divided into *gun*, or counties, and *si*, or smaller cities. Large metropolises are subdivided into *gu*, or districts, and *dong*, or neighborhoods. Each member who serves in a local government is elected by popular vote and serves a four-year term. The head of each local government can be reelected for up to three terms.

FOREIGN RELATIONS

South Korea maintains diplomatic relations with about 190 countries, including the United States and Canada. It has more than 100 embassies around the world that represent the interests of South Koreans by facilitating diplomatic relations, helping South Korean citizens who are traveling in other countries, and providing other services such as issuing passports and offering emergency aid when needed. The country also staffs 42 Korean Cultural Centers in 32 countries to promote South Korean food, music, sports, arts, and culture around the world.[7]

South Korean diplomat Ban Ki-moon, *right*, served as the UN secretary-general from 2007 to 2016. The secretary-general is the chief administrator of the UN.

Alongside many other countries, South Korea is a member of international organizations working toward the greater global good. South Korea became a member of the UN in 1991 and the Organization for Economic Co-operation and Development (OECD) in 1996. Other South Korean memberships include UNESCO; the World Health Organization (WHO); the International Atomic Energy Agency, which advocates for the peaceful use of nuclear power; and the Asia-Pacific Economic Cooperation, which promotes free trade in the Asia-Pacific region.

South Korea maintains a robust military in case conflicts arise. Since the Korean War, the US military has maintained a presence in South Korea to help the nation deter attacks from North Korea. In 2023 more than 28,000 US troops were stationed in South Korea.[8] After the 2022 presidential elections, President Yoon Suk-yeol said he resolved to strengthen political alliances with the United States, improve South Korea's ties with Japan, and make the country a "global pivotal state" that "advances freedom, peace, and prosperity through liberal democratic values and substantial cooperation."[9] As for its relationship with North Korea, the president vowed to strengthen South Korea's military defense against its neighbor to the north while still keeping dialogue open in the pursuit of a denuclearized North Korea in the future.

SOUTH KOREA'S MILITARY

South Korea's military is called the Republic of Korea Armed Forces. It consists of an army, navy, and air force. The biggest group is the army. The ROK Armed Forces has many responsibilities, the largest of which is defending the country from attack. All able-bodied men between 18 and 35 in South Korea must serve in the military for at least 18 to 21 months, depending on the branch.[10] They can delay the start of their service, but they must serve eventually. Other non-military matters of national security are covered by the country's National Intelligence Service. The Korean National Police Agency handles all civil and local policing.

CHAPTER **SEVEN**

ECONOMICS

Before 1960, South Korea's economy was small and agriculturally based. But over the next 60 years, it grew to become one of the largest economies in Asia—and the fourteenth largest in the world.[1] The nation's main trading partners are China, the United States, Japan, and Vietnam. Its exports include electrical machinery and semiconductors, petroleum, and automobiles. Some of South Korea's main natural resources are coal, tungsten, graphite, and lead.

In 2024 South Korea's economy was strong. Its workforce was large, educated, and skilled. In 2023 unemployment was relatively low, at 2.64 percent of the nation's population seeking a job. That year the country's gross domestic product (GDP) was approximately 1.7 trillion US dollars.[2]

The largest port in South Korea is in Busan. More than 60 percent of South Korea's imports and exports travel through this port.

THE CHAEBOL FAMILIES

Perhaps the biggest reason for South Korea's rapid rise to economic power is its chaebol system. The term is used to describe a highly selective group of families that have maintained control of South Korea's largest for-profit, non-governmental companies and have brought the country great wealth and economic standing. There are about 40 families in this system overall.[3] The five major families are the Lees of Samsung, the Koos of LG Corporation, the Cheys of SK Corporation, the Shins of Lotte Group, and the Chungs of Hyundai.

The legacies of these chaebol families date back to the armistice of 1953 that ended the Korean War. At the time, South Korea's military leaders gave a small group of men, who were the heads of important families, loans and financial backing to rebuild the South Korean economy from the ground up. Over the years, the companies run by these chaebol families expanded rapidly into different sectors, such as health care, credit cards, retail, and media. They became massive conglomerates that employed thousands of people. As more South Koreans were employed by these businesses, the companies made and exported

A TIGER ECONOMY

South Korea's rapid economic recovery after the Korean War is often called the Miracle on the Han River. Thanks to its leadership in production of electronic products and vehicles, the country also earned the reputation of being one of the four Asian countries and regions to experience something known as a tiger economy. The term *tiger economy* is inspired by the importance of tigers in Southeast Asian symbolism. Alongside Singapore, Hong Kong, and Taiwan, South Korea has achieved rapid economic success and poverty reduction through an emphasis on education, robust trading, increased exports in areas such as electronics and technology, and solid financial infrastructure.

more products. The companies increased wages, pushing living standards higher. From 2008 to 2023, the total sales of the five largest chaebol conglomerates in South Korea made up more than half of the country's GDP.[4]

Although the chaebol system turned South Korea into an economic superpower, the arrangement came with a cost. The chaebol families had close ties with some political figures, who let the families' power run unchecked for decades because they were so valuable to the economy. This attracted criticism from other world powers and South Korea's justice department.

Some political leaders and chaebol heads were punished for letting the arrangement get too out of hand. For example, President Park Geun-hye was removed from office in 2017 and sentenced to 20 years in prison for taking and soliciting bribes from Samsung, SK, and Lotte.

Shin Dong-bin was the chairman of Lotte Group. In 2018 he was sentenced to 30 months in prison in connection with Park Geun-hye's bribery case.

In 2023 LG announced a new home assistant robot. The company said the robot would use artificial intelligence to help customers with household tasks.

She was pardoned in 2021. Lee Jae-yong, chair of Samsung, was sentenced to a 2.5-year prison term as well.[5] Despite these occasional crackdowns, the chaebol system still thrives in South Korea.

INDUSTRY

The five major chaebol-run companies have helped shape South Korea's booming economy. LG Corporation originated in 1947 as a chemicals and plastics company. The Koo family increased the business's size and reach to include consumer electronics, telecommunications networks, cosmetics, and housewares. In 2005 LG split and formed a separate company called GS. This new conglomerate operates in the energy, retail, sports, and construction industries.

Samsung Electronics employs more than 300,000 people around the world. This is more than Apple and Google combined.[7]

Founded in 1938, Samsung Group began as a small business that exported fruits, dried fish, and other goods to China. Over the past 80 years, the company has expanded its reach to include electronics, insurance, shipbuilding, luxury hotels, hospitals, an amusement park, and a university. Its main group is Samsung Electronics, which produces goods such as refrigerators, washing machines, smartphones, tablets, and digital cameras. Samsung's business accounts for more than 14 percent of South Korea's GDP.[6]

When Hyundai opened its doors in 1947, it was a small construction business. Similarly to Samsung, Hyundai expanded its reach to include industries such as cars, electronics, shipbuilding, and financial products. Today, two of its biggest subsidiaries are Hyundai Motor Group, the third-largest carmaker in the world, and Hyundai Heavy Industries, the world's largest shipbuilding company.[8]

SK Group is made up of more than 175 companies, including SK Telecom, which is South Korea's largest wireless carrier. It serves nearly half of all South Koreans. But SK Group's biggest moneymaker is SK Hynix, a semiconductor company that is also the world's second-largest maker of memory chips.[9] Memory chips are found in almost all electronic devices, including computers, cell phones, and cars.

Founded in 1948, Lotte began as a chewing gum company, although it produces much more than gum. In addition to being the third-largest gum manufacturer in the world, Lotte makes other food products, runs discount and department stores, and has a chain of hotels and theme parks.[10] Lotte also includes companies in other industries, including finance, construction, energy, and electronics.

TRANSPORTATION

From planes and trains to automobiles, buses, and boats, there are many ways to get around in South Korea. With about 62,403 miles (100,428 km) of paved and unpaved roadways throughout the country, roads are the main means of transporting passengers and freight.[11] The first two freeways in South Korea were constructed in 1968. One connected Seoul to Incheon, just 21 miles (33 km) away. The other was a section of highway that stretched from Seoul to Suwon in the south.

It was the first part of a larger expressway that would eventually take travelers from Seoul to Busan, 201 miles (323 km) away.[12] Since 1968, a more modern, interconnected highway network has been built over time.

In addition to roadways, South Korea has a rail system that is both a commuter service and a long-distance means of travel. Five South Korean cities, including Seoul, Busan, Daejeon, Daegu, and Gwangju, operate subway systems, and all of the country's cities have extensive bus routes to bring people from home to work and elsewhere. The country's first high-speed rail line, called the Korea Train Express (KTX), was built in 2004. It connected Seoul and Busan. Today, the KTX also includes five other rail lines. These trains can whisk passengers from Seoul to Gyeongbu, Honam, Gyeongjeon, Jeolla, Gangneung, and many stops in between.

For locals and international visitors alike, South Korea has two major airports. Incheon International Airport is South Korea's largest airport and connects South Korea to destinations in dozens of countries around the world. Gimpo Airport, also near Seoul, has mostly domestic flights

AGING AND DIGITAL LITERACY

In 2023, 84 percent of South Korea's elderly population used smartphones.[13] But as modern technology keeps changing at a rapid rate, these same people have poorer digital literacy skills than their younger counterparts. As a result, South Korea has staffed free digital learning centers in Seoul and elsewhere. They provide digital education to senior citizens on topics such as booking tickets, comparing prices on various online platforms, and how to avoid falling victim to online scams. Though these centers faced budget cuts in 2024, they were seen as a way to help bridge the digital divide in the country.

but also has flights to China, Japan, and Taiwan. Beyond that, South Korea is home to several other smaller airports.

South Korea's main and biggest seaport is Busan. It is the fifth-largest port in the world.[14] Here, exports and imports are shuttled in and out of the country. Other large ports in South Korea include Ulsan, Incheon, and Gwangyang Hang.

COMMUNICATIONS INFRASTRUCTURE

For South Koreans, connecting to each other via the internet or a wireless cell phone provider is a seamless process even in rural areas. South Korea has widespread high-speed internet, and nearly all South Koreans have access. In 2024 almost all South Koreans used the internet at least occasionally.

A majority of people in South Korea have a cell phone too. With popular Samsung phones and 5G network subscriptions, South Koreans use their cell phones for many tasks, including communication, social media, work, and online shopping. In 2022 about 23 percent of smartphone users in the country interacted with their phones so much that they were considered to be dependent on their devices.[15]

Actors put on traditional performances at Incheon International Airport for passengers to enjoy before or after a flight. The airport also has attractions and art installations.

Portraits of several important leaders are featured on KRW bills. Shin Saimdang was a poet and painter who is featured on the 50,000 KRW bill.

CURRENCY

From buying daily goods to paying for monthly rent, South Koreans use a currency called the South Korean won (KRW). Paper money is printed in denominations of 1,000, 5,000, 10,000, and 50,000 won. Coins are minted in denominations of 1, 5, 10, 100, and 500 won, though 1 and 5 won coins are not widely used. In 2024, one US dollar was worth about 1,310 KRW.[16]

For international travelers looking to explore South Korea, there are a few important things to know when it comes to currency. A 10 percent value-added tax (VAT) is added to many goods sold throughout the country. Visitors can avoid the tax on purchases greater than 30,000 won when shopping in certified stores. Most popular stores are certified and will display a Tax Free sign. Visitors must ask for a tax refund check that can be redeemed at airport customs. Unlike in places such as the United States, tipping is not the norm in South Korea. However, many fancy restaurants and major hotels will add a 10 percent service charge on top of the 10 percent VAT.[17]

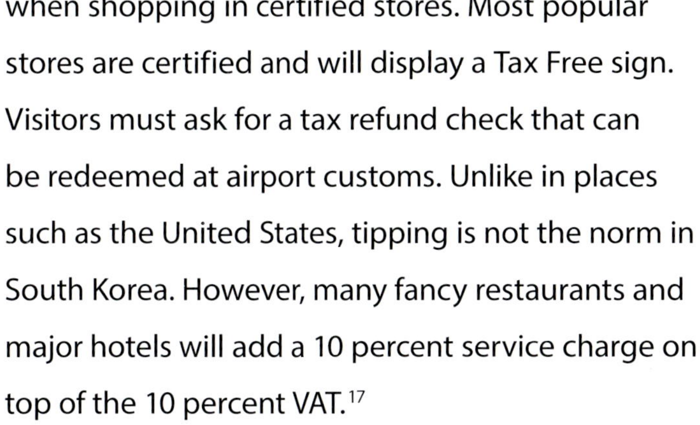

A LUXE TRAVELING EXPERIENCE

South Korea was the fourth country in the world to independently manufacture a high-speed train. By August 2023, more than one billion customers had ridden these trains since the KTX first started running in 2004. During that time, KTX trains from all of its lines had covered a combined 391 million miles (630 million km). That is enough to circle Earth 15,700 times. The total distance traveled by KTX passengers was 160.7 billion miles (258.6 billion km), or 1,724 times the distance between Earth and the sun.[18]

CHAPTER **EIGHT**

SOUTH KOREA TODAY

Today, South Korea is a country full of economic opportunities and ever-expanding horizons. But just because the country is turning into a tourist destination and its influence is increasing throughout the world doesn't mean it has discarded many of its long-held traditions. South Korea is a blend of old and new that is continuously evolving to meet the needs of today's changing world.

EDUCATION

In South Korea, which has one of the highest literacy rates in the world, education is viewed as a means to success. Elementary and middle school are free and mandatory for all South Koreans. In 2021 high school

Nightlife is an important part of the culture in large cities such as Seoul. Many businesses stay open late for food, dancing, shopping, and more.

Pressure for South Korean students to succeed and excel academically may start as early as elementary or middle school.

education became free as well, although it is not mandatory for all students. Specialized schools or elite private schools may charge tuition, however. After students' secondary school years, all South Korean citizens have the option of attending a college or university according to their academic abilities, regardless of their social status or class.

Typically, students begin school at the age of six. They spend six years in elementary school and three years in middle school. If students continue their education, they spend three years in high school and either four years at a university or two to three years at a junior college. Graduate study options are also available.

There are many types of high schools in South Korea, including regular public high schools, vocational high schools for hands-on learning, special-purpose high schools such as arts- or science-focused schools, and schools for gifted students. Some of the specialized or private schools require tuition fees, and all students must pass a qualification exam to get in. In 2022 the percentage of students who graduated high school and went on to college was 73.3 percent—the highest rate of college-bound graduates in any country.[1]

THE NURI CURRICULUM

In 2022 there were 8,562 kindergartens in South Korea.[2] Although early childhood education isn't required in the country, many families take advantage of the government's funding assistance to send their children to these programs. Children ages three to five are taught important skills from the Nuri Curriculum, a system adopted nationwide in 2013. They take part in physical exercise; learn how to communicate; and are given lessons on health and nutrition, building healthy social relationships, and expressing themselves artistically. Many classes involve going outside and interacting with nature.

Higher education institutions in South Korea vary in terms of program size and length. These include four-year general universities, online-only colleges meant for long-distance education, and junior colleges. In 2022 there were about 200 general four-year universities in South Korea that offered bachelor's degree programs.[3] Others are more career-specific, including schools meant for teachers, those created by companies to educate their employees, and polytechnic colleges meant for students hoping to learn job-related skills. In addition, six-year programs are available for students hoping to specialize in medicine, dentistry, or pharmaceutical careers.

FAMILY LIFE

In South Korea, family life is a huge part of the culture. Traditionally, Korean family hierarchies were defined by the Confucian conception of family relationships, with the man as the primary authority figure. Under this family model, the husband and father ruled the home and made all the important decisions in return for kindness and devotion from his wife and children. He spent most of his daily hours working and was the main income earner for the family. The mother mostly took care of cooking, childcare, and cleaning.

In some South Korean families today, this organizational structure is still the norm. In others, however, the relationship between family members is less strictly defined. In modern South Korea, many parents' ultimate goal is to see their children become successful. Consequently, children are often pushed to succeed academically and get into impressive schools. This immense pressure is often seen as an intense burden for many South Korean children today.

Although women are often still expected to shoulder the burden of childcare and homemaking, some South Korean women have chosen to focus on their careers instead of diving directly into motherhood. Others are choosing not to have children at all. Strict maternity leave policies at many workplaces make it nearly impossible for women to balance both a career and a family.

WORK-LIFE BALANCE

South Korea is known for its intense work culture. According to the OECD, South Korea has some of the highest working hours per week of any nation. Many young professionals feel pressured to work overtime in order to succeed in their careers.

In the early 2020s, President Yoon Suk-yeol proposed raising the maximum hours a person could work each week from 52 to 69. According to the government, this raise in overtime allotment was meant to allow seasonal workers such as delivery drivers, factory workers, and builders to work more hours and earn more money when they are most in demand. But many people, especially young people and workers in labor unions, objected to the policy. Protesters argued that the more hours they could theoretically work, the more pressure they would receive from their bosses and coworkers to stay late.

In the end, the South Korean government backed down on its proposal to increase the overtime limit, stating that extending overtime would be considered unhealthy.

In 2023 there were approximately 29.6 million workers in South Korea.[4]

Still, many South Koreans insist their work and recreation time are unbalanced, even if they don't meet the legal maximum of working hours. Often, employees are expected to attend mandatory after-work team dinners after an exhausting workday. Others feel duty bound to stay at the office until they see their boss leave, regardless of when they finish their job responsibilities. This overemphasis on work and productivity is one of the reasons South Korea has the highest suicide rate among developed countries in the OECD.[5]

However, this situation may be changing. In a sign of a growing generational divide, many people in South Korea's so-called MZ Generation, a local name for the millennials and young adults in Generation Z who make up about one-third of South Korea's population, are choosing a different path than the one their parents and grandparents took. Some are moving abroad for work. Others are choosing less lucrative careers, such as becoming musicians or artists, just so they don't have to work so many hours. "Even if they don't have a secure job, if they are able to pursue something that ignites their passion, they are willing to do that," says Cho Hee-kyung, a professor at the Hongik University College of Law.[6]

NAP CAFÉS

Work culture in South Korea is notorious for its many working hours and grueling days. To fill an ever-growing need, businesses called nap cafés have popped up in office buildings all over South Korea's major cities. Here, workers can find peace and quiet in dark rooms during their lunch breaks. Some customers lie down, while others sit in comfortable massage chairs. Nap cafés such as Mr. Healing Sleep Café in Seoul even have waitlists. "Workers, unless they work for big conglomerates, don't have spaces in their workplace where they can rest, unless they sleep on their desks," says Mr. Healing Sleep Café founder Ahn Sae-hee.[7]

Employees in some fields, such as video game development, felt that increasing maximum working hours could help them meet unpredictable deadlines.

RECREATION

A large portion of daily life in South Korea is occupied by family and work. But when South Koreans aren't at home or busy at the office, there are many popular activities to enjoy. Though many of them live in dense urban areas, South Koreans also love the outdoors. Many people enjoy hiking, and the 43 major public parks sprinkled around the country, 40 of which are in the mountains, are popular outdoor destinations.[8]

Baegundae is the highest peak in Bukhansan National Park. The popular trail to the top can become crowded.

One South Korean park, Bukhansan, has long held a world record as the national park with the highest number of visitors per square foot. More than six million people hike there each year.[9] Unlike in the United States, where hiking is often synonymous with solitude, many South Koreans prefer to hike in large groups and often with a guide. One popular hiking group is 4050 Seoul Metropolitan Mountain Club.

South Koreans looking to participate in other kinds of sports have plenty of options, including martial arts, sailing, and skiing. Thanks to the success of professional Korean golfers such as Ladies Professional Golf Association (LPGA) champ Park Se-ri, golf is a popular hobby. Dozens of golf courses dot the country, with many located in Seoul or on Jeju Island.

Outside the sports arena, singing and beauty play a big role in Korean society. A *noraebang* is a private room where groups of friends, dates, or coworkers go to sing, relieve stress, and have fun. These singing sanctuaries usually include large screens, wireless microphones, and a library of songs in multiple languages for karaoke.

Spas are a beloved tradition in South Korea too. Women and men alike go to spas to soak in

DATING IN SOUTH KOREA

Dating is an important part of South Korean culture, and there are many ways to do it. Many college students like to attend *kwa-tings*, or group blind date sessions between students from different campuses. Older potential couples prefer one-on-one dates called *mat-sun.* These are set up by either a friend or a professional matchmaking agency. Dating apps such as Wippy and NoonDate are popular too. The SKY People dating app is geared toward people who have attended top universities in South Korea or abroad.

hot tubs, get massages or body wraps, or treat themselves to facials. Many of the beauty products used at these spas have become popular around the world. Korean skin care products are known to be hydrating, high quality, and gentle on sensitive skin.

CHALLENGES AHEAD

Today, South Korea is one of the richest and most technologically advanced countries in the world. Its people love to work hard and enjoy themselves too. With delicious food, dozens of national parks, and enriching cultural traditions, the country has become a popular destination for tourists from across the globe.

But despite its status, South Korea is facing challenges ahead. Discrimination against women, members of the LGBTQ community, racial and ethnic minorities, and migrants and refugees is widespread in South Korea. In late 2015, demonstrations erupted across Seoul as people protested the government's mandate that all schools must use state-approved history books.

A large threat is the country's falling birth rate. South Korea's birth rate has been the lowest in the world since 2013. In 2023 it was 0.78 births per woman.[10] When combined with South Korea's rapidly aging population and the country's restrictive stance on immigration, the low birth rate could severely impact the country's economy because eventually there will be far fewer people who are able to work.

Since 2008 the South Korean government has spent more than $200 billion on programs to try to reverse the trend.[11] It has made paid paternity leave longer, offered money to new parents,

Climate change is a growing concern around the world. The South Korean activist group Youth 4 Climate Action led a protest in 2024 demanding government action.

Naejangsan National Park is one of the most popular tourist destinations in South Korea.

and launched social media campaigns to encourage men to help with childcare. But the low birth rate trend has continued. In 2024 President Yoon Suk-yeol announced the creation of a new government ministry that would try to do more to tackle the problem.

A FASCINATING COUNTRY

In the first half of 2024, more than 7.7 million foreign tourists visited South Korea. This was an increase of 74 percent from that same time period the year before.[12] The South Korean government plans to continue encouraging tourism, especially using the country's booming pop culture movement.

South Korea is a prosperous nation with a storied past. Tourists and locals alike enjoy its bustling metropolises and seaside ports. The nation will continue to be known for its majestic flora and fauna, serene spaces that calm the heart and mind, and mouth-watering cuisine.

ESSENTIAL **FACTS**

OFFICIAL NAME: REPUBLIC OF KOREA

GEOGRAPHY

Area: 38,502 square miles (99,720 sq km)

Highest Elevation: Mount Halla at 6,398 feet (1,950 m)

Lowest Elevation: Sea of Japan at 0 feet (0 m)

PEOPLE

Population: 52.1 million (2024 est.)

Most Populous City: Seoul (10 million)

Ethnic Groups: Korean, Japanese, Chinese

Religions: Protestantism, Buddhism, Catholicism, Confucianism, none, other

GOVERNMENT

Type of Government: Presidential republic

Capital: Seoul

Head of State and Government: President

Legislature: Unicameral, with a National Assembly

ECONOMY

Currency: South Korean won

Major Industries: Electronics, semiconductors, telecommunications, automobile manufacturing, shipbuilding, chemicals, steel

Natural Resources: Coal, tungsten, graphite, molybdenum, lead, hydropower

NATIONAL SYMBOLS

National Anthem: "Aegukga" ("The Patriotic Song")

National Flower: Mugunghwa

National Bird: Magpie

GLOSSARY

annex
To take a part of land or territory, typically by force.

appellate
Having the power to review the legal decisions of a lower court.

armistice
A temporary stop of fighting by mutual agreement.

brackish
Slightly salty, such as the conditions in the water where river and seawater mix in estuaries.

conglomerate
A large company made of many smaller parts, groups, or businesses.

constituency
A body of voters in a specific designated area who elect a representative to a legislative body.

estuary
An area where river water meets seawater.

floodplain
Land adjacent to a river that is subject to flooding.

gross domestic product (GDP)
The monetary value of all final goods and services produced within a nation's geographic borders over a specified period of time.

hierarchy
A ranked series within a group.

homogeneous
Made of parts that are the same kind.

impeachment
When someone is charged with misconduct while in office.

pagoda
A tower with many stories, each with its own roof, often built as part of a Buddhist temple.

subsidiary
A company that is owned and largely controlled by another company.

ADDITIONAL **RESOURCES**

SELECTED BIBLIOGRAPHY

Kim, Victoria, and Daisuke Wakabayashi. "What to Know about the Chaebol Families That Dominate South Korea's Economy." *New York Times*, 18 Dec. 2023, nytimes.com. Accessed 10 Oct. 2024.

Min Lee, Chung. "The Future of K-Power." *Carnegie Endowment for International Peace*, 22 Aug. 2024, carnegieendowment.org. Accessed 10 Oct. 2024.

"South Korea." *CIA World Factbook*, 15 Oct. 2024, cia.gov. Accessed 28 Oct. 2024.

FURTHER READINGS

Harper, Damian, et al. *Korea*. Lonely Planet, 2021.

Hello, South Korea. DK, 2023.

Huh, Aaron. *Simply Korean: Easy Recipes for Korean Favorites That Anyone Can Make*. DK, 2022.

ONLINE RESOURCES

To learn more about South Korea, please visit **abdobooklinks.com** or scan this QR code. These links are routinely monitored and updated to provide the most current information available.

MORE INFORMATION

For more information on this subject, contact or visit the following organizations:

Asian Art Museum

200 Larkin St.
San Francisco, CA 94102
asianart.org

The Asian Art Museum includes exhibits about all of Asia, including many galleries dedicated to South Korean culture.

Korean Cultural Center New York

333 East 32nd St.
New York, NY 10016
koreanculture.org

This Korean government organization provides an entryway to all things South Korea. It hosts diverse cultural and artistic activities, including gallery exhibitions, performing arts programs, film festivals, educational workshops, and more.

Ministry of Foreign Affairs

60, Sajik-ro 8-gil, Jongno-gu
Seoul, Republic of Korea 03172
mofa.go.kr

The Republic of South Korea's Ministry of Foreign Affairs shares information about life in South Korea on its website. The site provides an overview of Korean culture, history, and daily life.

SOURCE **NOTES**

CHAPTER 1. A TOUR OF SOUTH KOREA

1. "Gyeongbokgung Palace Tickets and Changing of the Guard Hours." *Agoda*, 12 Dec. 2023, agoda.com. Accessed 30 Dec. 2024.
2. Hahna Yoon. "How to Get Around Seoul." *Lonely Planet*, 10 Feb. 2024, lonelyplanet.com. Accessed 30 Dec. 2024.
3. "Bukchon Hanok Village." *US News*, n.d., travel.usnews.com. Accessed 30 Dec. 2024.
4. "Bukchon Hanok Village." *Hotels.com*, n.d., hotels.com. Accessed 30 Dec. 2024.
5. "About Seoul Sky." *Seoul Sky*, n.d., seoulsky.lotteworld.com. Accessed 30 Dec. 2024.
6. "Seoul Lantern Festival." *Seoul Tourism Organization*, n.d., sto.or.kr. Accessed 30 Dec. 2024.
7. Heather Chen and Sooyoung Rhee. "A Seoul Neighborhood Is So Crowded with Tourists That the Government Is Taking Over." *CNN*, 11 July 2024, cnn.com. Accessed 30 Dec. 2024.
8. "Dongdaemun Market." *US News*, n.d., travel.usnews.com. Accessed 30 Dec. 2024.
9. "Bukhansan National Park." *US News*, n.d., travel.usnews.com. Accessed 30 Dec. 2024.

CHAPTER 2. GEOGRAPHY

1. David J. Nemeth. "The Geography of the Koreas." *Asia Society*, n.d., asiasociety.org. Accessed 30 Dec. 2024.
2. "South Korea." *CIA World Factbook*, 15 Oct. 2024, cia.gov. Accessed 30 Dec. 2024.
3. Bae-ho Hahn et al. "South Korea." *Britannica*, 30 Dec. 2024, britannica.com. Accessed 30 Dec. 2024.
4. "South Korea," *CIA World Factbook*.
5. Bae-ho et al., "South Korea."
6. "Korea's National Parks." *Peaks and Penguins*, n.d., peaksandpenguins.com. Accessed 30 Dec. 2024.
7. Ann Babe. "Best 6 National Parks in South Korea." *Lonely Planet*, 6 July 2022, lonelyplanet.com. Accessed 30 Dec. 2024.
8. Bae-ho et al., "South Korea."
9. Nemeth, "Geography of the Koreas."
10. "South Korea," *CIA World Factbook*.
11. "Jeju Island." *New 7 Wonders of Nature*, n.d., nature.new7wonders.com. Accessed 30 Dec. 2024.
12. Violet Kim, Gigi Ban, and Sunny Kim. "33 Gorgeous Islands Await You in South Korea." *CNN Travel*, 9 Nov. 2017, cnn.com. Accessed 30 Dec. 2024.
13. Kim, Ban, and Kim. "33 Gorgeous Islands."
14. L. Yoon. "Weather and Climate in South Korea." *Statista*, 18 Oct. 2024, statista.com. Accessed 30 Dec. 2024.
15. Yoon, "Weather and Climate."
16. L. Yoon. "Duration of Yellow Dust in South Korea from 2012 to 2023." *Statista*, 18 Oct. 2024, statista.com. Accessed 30 Dec. 2024.

CHAPTER 3. PLANTS AND ANIMALS

1. Jackie De Burca. "Biodiversity." *Constructive Voices*, 26 Feb. 2024, constructive-voices.com. Accessed 30 Dec. 2024.
2. Bae-ho Hahn et al. "South Korea." *Britannica*, 30 Dec. 2024, britannica.com. Accessed 30 Dec. 2024.
3. Yong Kwon. "South Korea's Reforestation Campaign." *Diplomat*, 1 Nov. 2021, thediplomat.com. Accessed 30 Dec. 2024.
4. "Distribution of Korean Red Pine." *National Atlas of Korea II*, n.d., nationalatlas.ngii.go.kr. Accessed 30 Dec. 2024.
5. "Endangered Wild Plant Species." *National Atlas of Korea II*, n.d., nationalatlas.ngii.go.kr. Accessed 30 Dec. 2024.

6. Isaac Lee and Leila Sackur. "No Go for Humans but Wildlife Finds Sanctuary in DMZ Between North and South Korea." *NBC News*, 25 Feb. 2023, nbcnews.com. Accessed 30 Dec. 2024.
7. Lisha Pace. "Animals in South Korea." *AZ Animals*, 4 Mar. 2023, a-z-animals.com. Accessed 30 Dec. 2024.
8. "Asian Giant Hornet." *Missouri Department of Agriculture*, n.d., agriculture.mo.gov. Accessed 30 Dec. 2024.
9. James Watuwa. "Comma (*Polygonia c-album*)." *Butterfly Identification*, 29 Aug. 2018, butterflyidentification.com. Accessed 30 Dec. 2024.
10. "Representative Wild Birds." *National Atlas of Korea II*, n.d., nationalatlas.ngii.go.kr. Accessed 30 Dec. 2024.
11. Anna Jeanine Kim. "South Korea Is a Test Case on How to Fight an Ecological Disaster." *National Geographic*, 15 Aug. 2023, nationalgeographic.com. Accessed 30 Dec. 2024.
12. George Berry. "Last Captive Indo-Pacific Bottlenose Dolphin to Be Freed in South Korea." *Whale and Dolphin Conservation*, 8 Aug. 2022, uk.whales.org. Accessed 30 Dec. 2024.
13. "Magpie." *AZ Animals*, 27 May 2024, a-z-animals.com. Accessed 30 Dec. 2024.

CHAPTER 4. HISTORY

1. "Korean War." *History.com*, 11 May 2022, history.com. Accessed 30 Dec. 2024.
2. Aaron O'Neill. "The Korean War." *Statista*, 26 Aug. 2024, statista.com. Accessed 30 Dec. 2024.
3. "Government." *Prime Minister's Secretariat*, n.d., opm.go.kr. Accessed 30 Dec. 2024.
4. Chong-suk Han. "Gwangju Uprising." *Britannica*, 11 Dec. 2024, britannica.com. Accessed 30 Dec. 2024.
5. Se Young Jang. "The Gwangju Uprising." *Wilson Center*, 17 July 2017, wilsoncenter.org. Accessed 30 Dec. 2024.
6. "South Korea." *CIA World Factbook*, 15 Oct. 2024, cia.gov. Accessed 30 Dec. 2024.
7. "An Audacious Initiative." *Korean Cultural Center New York*, n.d., koreanculturalcenter.org. Accessed 30 Dec. 2024.
8. "South Korea."

CHAPTER 5. PEOPLE AND CULTURE

1. "South Korea." *CIA World Factbook*, 15 Oct. 2024, cia.gov. Accessed 30 Dec. 2024.
2. "South Korea."
3. "Diversity in Seoul." *Council on International Educational Exchange*, n.d., ciee.org. Accessed 30 Dec. 2024.
4. "Korean." *University of North Carolina*, n.d., asianstudies.unc.edu. Accessed 30 Dec. 2024.
5. "South Korea."
6. "Bongeunsa Temple." *Seoul Guide*, 17 Dec. 2021, theseoulguide.com. Accessed 30 Dec. 2024.
7. L. Yoon. "Religion in South Korea." *Statista*, 14 Oct. 2024, statista.com. Accessed 30 Dec. 2024.
8. "South Korea."
9. Tim Adams. "K-Everything: The Rise and Rise of Korean Culture." *Guardian*, 4 Sept. 2022, theguardian.com. Accessed 30 Dec. 2024.
10. Philip Merrill. "BTS Become First K-Pop Band to Debut at No. 1 on *Billboard* 200." *Grammy Awards*, 29 May 2018, grammy.com. Accessed 30 Dec. 2024.
11. "*Parasite*: Awards." *IMDb*, n.d., imdb.com. Accessed 30 Dec. 2024.
12. "World Taekwondo Celebrate 25 Years on the Olympic Programme." *World Taekwondo*, n.d., m.worldtaekwondo.org. Accessed 30 Dec. 2024.

SOURCE **NOTES** CONTINUED

CHAPTER 6. POLITICS

1. Rosie Pentreath. "What Is South Korea's National Anthem and What Are the Lyrics?" *Classic FM*, 28 Nov. 2022, classicfm.com. Accessed 30 Dec. 2024.
2. Pauliina Majasaari. "South Korea National Assembly Elections 2024." *Global Human Rights Defence*, 12 Apr. 2024, ghrd.org. Accessed 30 Dec. 2024.
3. Victor Cha, Jinwan Park, and Andy Lim. "South Korea's 2024 General Election." *Center for Strategic and International Studies*, 10 Apr. 2024, csis.org. Accessed 30 Dec. 2024.
4. L. Yoon. "Results of the 20th Presidential Election in South Korea in 2022." *Statista*, 25 June 2024, statista.com. Accessed 30 Dec. 2024.
5. Cha, Park, and Lim, "South Korea's 2024 General Election."
6. Michael Ray. "Moon Jae-In." *Britannica*, 14 Dec. 2024, britannica.com. Accessed 30 Dec. 2024.
7. "Constitution." *Korean Cultural Center New York*, n.d., koreanculture.org. Accessed 30 Dec. 2024.
8. Caitlin Campbell and Christina L. Arabia. "US–South Korea Alliance: Issues for Congress." *Congressional Research Service*, 12 Sept. 2023, crsreports.congress.gov. Accessed 16 Jan. 2025.
9. Scott A. Snyder. "How South Korea's Foreign Policy Could Change Under the New President." *Council on Foreign Relations*, 10 Mar. 2022, cfr.org. Accessed 30 Dec. 2024.
10. "South Korea." *CIA World Factbook*, 15 Oct. 2024, cia.gov. Accessed 30 Jan. 2025.

CHAPTER 7. ECONOMICS

1. Françoise Huang. "South Korea." *Allianz Trade*, Nov. 2024, allianz-trade.com. Accessed 30 Dec. 2024.
2. "South Korea." *CIA World Factbook*, 15 Oct. 2024, cia.gov. Accessed 30 Dec. 2024.
3. Eleanor Albert. "South Korea's Chaebol Challenge." *Council on Foreign Relations*, 4 May 2018, cfr.org. Accessed 30 Dec. 2024.
4. Victoria Kim and Daisuke Wakabayashi. "What to Know about the Chaebol Families That Dominate South Korea's Economy." *New York Times*, 18 Dec. 2023, nytimes.com. Accessed 30 Dec. 2024.
5. Kim and Wakabayashi, "What to Know."
6. Albert, "Chaebol Challenge."
7. Albert, "Chaebol Challenge."
8. Albert, "Chaebol Challenge."
9. Albert, "Chaebol Challenge."
10. Albert, "Chaebol Challenge."
11. "South Korea," *CIA World Factbook*.
12. Matt VanVolkenburg. "Korea Enters 'Highway Age' 50 Years Ago." *Korea Times*, 23 Feb. 2021, koreatimes.co.kr. Accessed 30 Dec. 2024.

13. Kim Yeon-joong. "Elderly South Koreans Face Digital Isolation as Government Slashes Tech Budget." *Korea Pro*, 26 Apr. 2024, koreapro.org. Accessed 30 Dec. 2024.
14. "Busan Port." *Silver Runner*, n.d., silver-runner.com. Accessed 30 Dec. 2024.
15. "Ownership Rate of Smartphones in South Korea from 2011 to 2023." *Statista*, 10 May 2024, statista.com. Accessed 30 Dec. 2024.
16. "South Korean Won to US Dollar Spot Exchange Rate." *Federal Reserve Bank of Saint Louis*, 3 Jan. 2024, fred.stlouisfed.org. Accessed 30 Dec. 2024.
17. "Money." *Visit Seoul*, n.d., english.visitseoul.net. Accessed 30 Dec. 2024.
18. Wu Jinhua and Lee Kyoung Mi. "Bullet Train KTX Marks 20th Anniversary with Billionth User." *Korea.net*, 1 Apr. 2024, korea.net. Accessed 30 Dec. 2024.

CHAPTER 8. SOUTH KOREA TODAY

1. "Early Childhood Education." *Ministry of Education*, n.d., english.moe.go.kr. Accessed 30 Dec. 2024.
2. "Early Childhood Education."
3. "Early Childhood Education."
4. "South Korea." *CIA World Factbook*, 15 Oct. 2024, cia.gov. Accessed 16 Jan. 2025.
5. Josh Lederman. "A 69-Hour Workweek? That's No Way to Live, Young South Koreans Say." *NBC News*, 22 Mar. 2023, nbcnews.com. Accessed 30 Dec. 2024.
6. Lederman, "A 69-Hour Workweek?"
7. Lederman, "A 69-Hour Workweek?"
8. Scott Yorko. "What Could Americans Learn from the Way Koreans Hike?" *Backpacker*, 4 Dec. 2024, backpacker.com. Accessed 30 Dec. 2024.
9. Yorko, "What Could Americans Learn?"
10. Ashley Ahn. "South Korea Has the World's Lowest Fertility Rate, a Struggle with Lessons for Us All." *National Public Radio*, 19 Mar. 2023, npr.org. Accessed 30 Dec. 2024.
11. Jessie Yeung. "South Korea's Birth Rate Is So Low, the President Wants to Create a Ministry to Tackle It." *CNN*, 9 May 2024, cnn.com. Accessed 31 Jan. 2025.
12. Peden Doma Bhutia. "Korean Wave Makes a Splash with 7.7 Million Tourists as China Leads the Tourism Charge." *Skift*, 30 July 2024, skift.com. Accessed 30 Dec. 2024.

INDEX

ABOUT THE **AUTHOR**

ALEXIS BURLING

Alexis Burling has written dozens of articles and books for young readers on a variety of topics including current events, biographies of famous people, nutrition and fitness, careers, and money management. She is also a professional book critic with reviews of adult and young adult books, author interviews, and other publishing industry–related articles appearing in the *New York Times*, *Washington Post Book World*, *San Francisco Chronicle*, and more. Alexis lives in Washington with her husband and cats.